AFRICAN POLITICAL, ECONOMIC AND SECURITY ISSUES

EDUCATION FOR THE NEW FRONTIER: RACE, EDUCATION AND TRIUMPH IN JIM CROW AMERICA (1867-1945)

AFRICAN POLITICAL, ECONOMIC AND SECURITY ISSUES

Additional books in this series can be found on Nova's website
under the Series tab.

Additional E-books in this series can be found on Nova's website
under the E-books tab.

EDUCATION FOR THE NEW FRONTIER: RACE, EDUCATION AND TRIUMPH IN JIM CROW AMERICA (1867-1945)

GREG WIGGAN
EDITOR

Nova Science Publishers, Inc.
New York

NOTICE TO THE READER

Library of Congress Cataloging-in-Publication Data

Education for the new frontier : race, education and triumph in Jim Crow
America (1867-1945) / editor, Greg Wiggan.
    p. cm.
Includes bibliographical references and index.
ISBN 978-1-61209-673-5 (softcover : alk. paper)
1. African American children--Education--History--20th century. 2.
Segregation in education--Southern States--History. 3. United States--Race
relations--History--20th century. 4. African Americans--Civil rights. I.
Wiggan, Greg A., 1976-
    LC2741.E37 2011
    371.829'96073--dc22
                                2011009056

Published by Nova Science Publishers, Inc. ✛ *New York*

CONTENTS

Acknowledgments   vii

Introduction: Social and Historical Context of Education   ix

Chapter 1   Education for Freedom: Atlanta University
                  and Its Social Significance During and After
                  the Reconstruction Period, 1867-1910   1
                  Greg Wiggan

Chapter 2   Straddler No More: Kelly Miller and the Fight
                  Over Black Education in the Age
                  of Booker T. Washington, 1895-1915   31
                  Sylvie Coulibaly

Chapter 3   Education and the Intelligence Assessment
                  of African Americans, 1917 – 1945   53
                  Cameron Seay

About the Authors   91

Index   93

ACKNOWLEDGMENTS

I wish to thank my very first teacher, Mrs. Lyons, the renowned educator in Sav-la-Mar, Westmoreland, Jamaica, and my last teacher, the master teacher and high priest, Dr. Asa Hilliard. I owe my deepest gratitude to these two educators who have had a profound impact on my growth and development. I also wish to thank my mother and father (and brother Robby), who taught me to be firm even when faced by institutional racism and prejudice. And to the 'Vicker,' elder ancestor Errol Peynado, and the queen mothers, Mama Scott and Mama "P," and to the late Mr. Clinton Scarlett, who was the top librarian in Sav-la-Mar for at least three decades, blessed love.

In loving memory of the Jegna, Dr. John Henrik Clarke.

INTRODUCTION: SOCIAL AND HISTORICAL CONTEXT OF EDUCATION

As we approach the end of the first decade in the 21st century, it is important to pause and reflect on the events and developments of the last century that have impacted our progress and social thinking in education and the larger society. In the Caribbean and African Diasporic scenery, the 2010 year ascribed the passing of two giant scholars: Rhodes Scholar Rex Nettleford, one of whose best-known works *is Mirror, Mirror: Identity, Race and Protest in Jamaica,* and Barry Chevannes, known for his work *Rastafari: Roots and Ideology,* among others; both transitioned during this year. The passing of these two scholars has left a great void in the field, and simultaneously, a greater recognition and celebration for the body of work that these researchers have produced. Nettleford and Chevannes will have their place in history as two of the most important scholars in the post-independence or neocolonial era of Caribbean history (since Frantz Fanon and Walter Rodney). Nettleford was Vice Chancellor emeritus of the University of the West Indies (UWI), Mona, and Chevannes was the former Dean of the Faculty of Social Sciences at the University.

Researchers have acknowledged that the Caribbean and Central and South America are important gateways for understanding the history of the Transatlantic slave trade and the experiences of Africans in the Diaspora, since the Caribbean islands are where the first African slaves were taken. In 1619, Dutch slave traders took slaves from the island of Barbados to James Town, Virginia in North America. The historical connection between blacks in the Caribbean and North America can be found in some of the early college graduates, as John Russwurm from Jamaica was one of the first blacks to receive a college education in North America. In 1826, Russwurm graduated from Bowdoin College and later went to Liberia as part of the American Colonization Society's effort to establish a colony in West Africa. Later on, Edward Wilmot Blyden, who was from the island of Saint Thomas, Virgin Islands, came to North America and like Russwurm, he too went to Liberia where he later became President of the Liberia College. Blyden is known for his pioneering work in the manuscripts, *Christianity, Islam and the Negro Race* and *African Life and Customs*. William Henry Crogman, who graduated from Atlanta University in the class of 1876, was from the Caribbean island of Saint Martin and he later became the first president of Clark University in Atlanta, Georgia, from 1903-1910 (see chapter 1 of this book). W. E. B. Du Bois, who was one of the most important and outstanding intellectuals of the 20th century, could trace his ancestry to Haiti, and Malcolm X, who was one of the brilliant and iconic social leaders of his time, explained his connection to the Caribbean through his Grenadian mother. In the case of St. Clair Drake, the renowned educator of Stanford and Roosevelt Universities, he was the son of Barbadian parents. Much of this has been investigated in *Holding Aloft the Banner of the Ethiopia*, where Winston James explains the historical connection between the Caribbean islands and North America and the production of public scholars and black leadership in the U.S.

In the history of the Americas, it is generally accepted that the first inhabitants of the region appeared more than 50,000 years ago. These indigenous groups populated North and South America and they developed unique cultures (language, religion, and group practices) and civilizations. Some of the ethnic groups that emerged in the Americas were the Olmecs, Aztecs, Mayans, Caribs, Tainos, Chibchas, Tupis, Guaranis, Incas, Araucanians, and the Arawaks, among others. Lesley-Gail Atkinson has edited an excellent collection of works on the Tainos entitled, *The Earliest Inhabitants: The Dynamics of the Jamaican Taino*. Like the Tainos, the other indigenous groups created civilizations that flourished in Guatemala, Mexico, Chile, Paraguay, Argentina, the Caribbean islands, and North America. I remember as a little boy asking my grandmother if she could take me to see some of the Arawaks.[1] She looked me in the eyes and let me down gently, she said, 'me grandson, I would love to carry you to show you dem, but dem no

---

[1]During this time of Jamaican history, the words Arawak and Taino were used interchangeably. However, modern research has revealed that these were indeed two different ethnic groups.

longer alive in Jamaica.'[2] Seeing the rather puzzled and distraught look on her grandson's face, and sensing a great level of disappointment, she said, 'let me tell you how dem did stay.'[3]

Around the time of the Arawaks, Africans also made voyages to Central and South America long before Christopher Columbus came to the region, and they created a civilization among the Olmecs and left artifacts, sculptures (busts), and monuments that have been discovered by modern researchers (see Ivan Van Sertima's *They Came Before Columbus*). The large Olmec busts can be found in Mexico, as well as throughout Central and South America. The Olmecs had distinct African features and practices, and as an ethnic group, they predated the arrival of European explorers in the Americas.

The indigenous groups that lived in Central and South America were highly sophisticated and civilized, and they had their own social, economic, and religious systems. However, all of these creations they would lose in the 1400s when the Portuguese and Spanish began to colonize and enslave the people of the region. The Portuguese and Spanish came to the Caribbean, and Central and South America with gunpowder, guns, and other advanced military conventions. They began to conquer the native population by force and, more importantly, through social and ideological control – the former being the most advanced and effective form of hegemonic domination. European colonizers and missionaries would demonize the indigenous groups and rewrite history to suggest that they had no systems of education, and that they were uncivilized 'pagans.' After the indigenous populations began to die out because of diseases like smallpox and tuberculosis, which the Europeans introduced into the region, and because of the brutal treatment on the plantations, the colonialists began to import Africans. The first slaves from Africa were shipped directly to the Caribbean where they were forced to do some of the most gruesome work to create wealth for the Spanish and Portuguese empires (see Eric Williams' *Documents of West Indian History*, *Capitalism and Slavery*, and *From Columbus to Castro*). The Arabs initiated the slave trade before the Europeans. However, the Europeans would master it and expand it around the globe. In the Arab slave trade, Islam became the official religion of the conquered people and territories, and the Qur'an became the authorized holy book in these captive lands. Africans who were invaded by Arabs were forced to adopt the new religion. In the 1400s, when

---

[2]From Jamaican patois (Patwa) to Standard English, this statement is interpreted as, "my grandson, I wish I could take you to see them (Arawaks), but they are no longer alive on the island of Jamaica."

[3]This statement is interpreted as saying, "let me tell you some things about them (Arawaks)."

the European explorers entered the west coast of Africa seeking spices and to trade gold, they were amazed by what they saw in the place they called the Gold Coast of Africa (Ghana). Not only would they embark on a trade in gold, they would ultimately negotiate with the Arabs and to a lesser extent with dissenting tribal groups, to get a steady supply of Africans to work as free laborers in the Americas.

During this time, the Roman Catholic Pope acted as the global arbitrator over disputes in the European colonial territories. For example, in the Treaty of Tordesillas of 1494, Pope Alexander VI ended a dispute in the Americas over colonial territories by dividing up land among the Spanish and Portuguese. Both countries paid tithes to the Roman Catholic Church – making it the most wealthy and powerful religious institution in the world. Later, Martin Luther's Protestant Reformation movement challenged the Catholic Church and its teachings, as well as its religious authority and social oppression. However, the Pope and the Church would have no part of that, and in the Council of Trent, the Pope attempted to suppress the new denomination that was emerging from Luther's questioning, and what the Vatican considered as unauthorized interpretations of the Bible. From the entrance of Christopher Columbus into the Americas in 1492, after the Columbus era under Spain's direction, Hernán Cortés entered Mexico and began a conquest that toppled the Aztecs and expanded the Spanish colonial empire — creating wealth and power that made the country elite amongst European nations. Seeing the success of the Spanish and Portuguese, the British entered the slave trade. Later in the 1600s, the British would battle the Spanish and emerge as the supreme colonial power under Queen Elizabeth I (through the expeditions of Captain John Hawkins) and then King Stuart James.

King James timed the publication of his version of the Bible for the maximum effect on his colonial empire, where all the slaves in the empire would learn theology from his authorized version, which was a departure from the literature that the Roman Catholic Church was using in the Spanish and Portuguese colonies. Religious pilgrimage and crusading ran concurrently with colonization, as missionaries were used to introduce the indigenous groups to new Gods as part of their slave identities, and to teach them how to be obedient and acculturate to colonial life. Religious indoctrination taught slaves not to think but to believe. Missionaries and slave masters knew that a thinking slave who had historical knowledge would challenge and perhaps dismantle the system of slavery. Therefore, the missionaries and the colonialists envisioned a one-world religion, and they often felt that it was their duty to proselytize and make sure that everyone had the same beliefs about God, which were premised on servitude and obedience.

In doing so, these missionaries labeled indigenous cultural groups as heathens and 'pagans,' even though they were themselves historical contemporaries to these older groups who developed their own cultures, civilizations, and God concepts long before the Spanish, Portuguese, and the British. Through the persistent struggles of Maroons (run-away Africans and slaves) and many slave revolts, the enslaved and colonized were able to see the light of freedom (See Bev Carey's *Story of the Maroon*). These same freedom fighters were found in Spanish colonies as well, and they were referred to as *cimarrones*. In North America, many maroons were found in Virginia and the Carolinas (see Hugo Leaming's work, *Hidden Americans: Maroons of Virginia and the Carolinas*). On the continent of Africa, the Zulu warriors waged some of the most successful and sustained battles against the colonial forces. They were some of the most feared and revered freedom fighters — a terror to the European forces. The fight for independence culminated in 1803 when Haiti was successful in defeating the French to become the first free black Republic in the world (see *The Black Jacobins* by C.L.R. James).

There was still much work to do in the way of decolonization because one of the results of colonialism was the creation of a social caste system where the indigenous and slave populations that intermixed with the white colonialists, either by force or consent (in most cases by force), produced racially and ethnically mixed offspring who enjoyed greater social privileges from the colonialists over their non-racially mixed peers. For example, when Hernán Cortés came to Mexico he chose a young Mayan slave girl known as Malinche as his translator and sexual servant. Cortés had Malinche baptized Dona Maria and he later had a child with her named Don Martin Cortés, who was now a part of a social class called the mestizos (see Norton et al. *A People and a Nation*). Due to the fact that the mestizos were visibly racially mixed, they were in a higher social class than their enslaved indigenous counterparts. This essentially created a social hierarchy in the slave quarters and society, where to have some European features and ethos was a passage to a better life. As part of white supremacist ideology, a "mulatto hypothesis" was developed, which suggested that lighter complexioned blacks or Native Americans were superior and more intelligent than their darker-skinned peers because they had more "white blood" in them. The dilemma surrounding black or dark complexion was such a pervasive issue, that even in the neo-colonial era, black heads of states were generally racially mixed. The racialization of blacks is addressed in chapter 1 as it relates to black college admissions practices, and to a greater extent in chapter 3, which investigates the intelligence testing of African Americans and its connection to American education.

The mestizo, mulatto and other racially mixed groups were a social hybrid of the indigenous or African descent populations, and the colonialists. The colonialists would give these racially mixed children a higher social ranking than their darker-skinned peers, and they were often even allowed to attend one of the schools that was setup by the Catholic Church. They could even hold high positions in the society and most considered themselves to be racially different, and therefore entitled to greater social privileges among the colonized. Through white supremacist ideology, colonization and racial intermixing created intra-group racial discrimination and social legacies that continue to this present day, where skin bleaching is still a problem in the Caribbean, Central and South America, and throughout the continent of Africa. In the late 1800s, as Chinese and East Indian indentured laborers were brought to the Caribbean and Central and South America, they added to the rich cultural diversity of the region. However, even with this interchange of cultures and group intermixing, it was understood that to have dark-skin and African features would carry the greatest social stigma and discrimination. Furthermore, African customs and spirituality were the most demonized practices and belittled ethos in the region, and this was also true in the rest of the world. To this present day, retentions of African spirituality in the Americas are often referred to as Voodoo and Obadiah, words that conjure up fear and negative images, and Christian churches that practice spirit dancing and spirit possession (later called the holy spirit possession) are considered primitive and backward forms of worship. In the slave quarters of the Caribbean and Americas, the Yoruba deities that the Africans brought with them to the region were disguised and synchronized as Catholic saints in church. For example, the deity Oduduwa is often synchronized as Saint Manuel and Oshanla is synchronized with Saint Ann in Catholicism. The Africans made the new religion work for them by incorporating aspects of their native spirituality. However, African drums were prohibited in church worship for fear that they would be used to send messages among slaves and to invoke the African deities. The slaves developed a unique way of stomping their feet and clapping their hands as a rhythmic drum, while they used the call and response singing as a central aspect of praise and worship (This tradition can still be found in many African American churches in the South of the U.S.). The call and response singing was also important for coping and keeping daily inspiration, while enduring the horrific plantation life as a free laborer. On the plantations of the Americas, this is how Africans retained much of their spirituality. Even today, Brazil has more Yoruba worshipers (synchronized with the Catholic saints) than perhaps anywhere in the world – this includes Nigeria, where most people have been converted to Islam and Christianity because of crusading, slavery, and colonialism.[4] While each religion has its own merit, the point here is to explain how the indigenous groups' beliefs and practices evolved and even became stigmatized because of slavery (Islamic and Christian) and crusading.

The colonialists were successful in creating a pretext for slavery by suggesting that Africans were like savages and therefore God gave them the right to enslave indigenous people and take their land and civilize them with Christianity. This was such an effective form of legitimation and social control, that one can still hear the progeny of colonized people and slaves giving thanks for their ancestors' enslavement, because it apparently gave them the right religion and brought them 'salvation' in time. This is rather disheartening, but perhaps it also helps us to understand how on some of the Caribbean islands where the slaves and indigenous populations outnumbered the colonialists 8 to 1, why they remained docile and obedient even when there were no guns in sight. Clearly, the initial brute force of colonialism was usurped by the pervasive ideological control mechanism that was used to ensure the continued enslavement and dehumanization of the oppressed.

In the North American context, the Native Americans and Africans were subject to a similar campaign of cultural genocide and de-humanization. For colonizers and enslavers, because the native populations were not considered to be fully humans, it was okay to destroy them, take their land, and use their women for sexual pleasures. Like the slave uprisings of the Caribbean and Central and South America, the slave revolts in North America were aimed at gaining freedom, access to education, and equal opportunity. The revolts led by Gabriel Prosser in 1800, Denmark Vesey in 1822 (Vesey was originally from the Caribbean island of Saint Thomas) and the notorious Nat Turner rebellion of 1831 were all human sacrifices that sought to dismantle slavery and to give future generations an opportunity to live as free human beings. Nat Turner's revolt overlaps with the Sam Sharpe revolt in Jamaica, which ultimately led to the abolition of slavery on the island. Visitors can still find a sculpture of Sam Sharpe in the middle of Montego Bay square in Jamaica, where they can see 'Daddy Sharpe' as he is affectionately called. After the Sam Sharpe and Nat Turner revolts, and the independence of Haiti, there was a

---

[4]Brazil was Portugal's most vital colony, where it imported millions of Africans. As a result, Brazil's African descent population is unrivaled in the Americas. As time progressed, they masterfully weaved in the Yoruba deities into the Catholic Church traditions.

general fear among slaveholders that slaves were learning of these armed struggles for freedom and that more revolts would follow.

Towards this end, in North America during the 1830s and 1840s, Horace Mann campaigned for a common school, which he viewed as being crucial for the development and maintenance of a democratic society. Mann argued that education was needed to sustain a democratic society and that this was necessary for equal participation and for citizens to share basic democratic principles. He believed that a common moral education would help to decrease social deviance and inequality in the society. However, as schools were gradually being created, usually they were not for slaves. For fear of uprisings and competition, generally no one wanted to educate a slave to be a critical thinker or to have an understanding of history or a collective cultural identity, because this would be a dangerous undertaking in regards to the preservation of group domination and the advancement of a capitalist society. In his book *Capitalism and Slavery*, Eric Williams has done some excellent research on this topic.

In the history of the U.S., there has been a struggle to maintain a dominant cultural and religious identity, which affects schools. A white Protestant identity was essential to an American identity, and this was perceived as a threat by members of the Roman Catholic Church. A white Protestant identity was an even greater challenge to Africans, African Americans, and Native Americans. While the Irish, Jewish, and Italian immigrants were eventually able to fully assimilate into a dominant white identity, this was a greater challenge for racial minority groups who were unable to alter their appearance (phenotype) enough to assimilate into the dominant white cultural identity. One drop of African blood meant that a person was black, a pronouncement that carried a stigma and negative social consequences with burdens that were too heavy to bear. The irony is that all human beings share a common origin, Africa, and all human beings have "African blood" in them. For indeed, human beings share 99.9% of the same Deoxyribonucleic acid [DNA]. However, in order to maintain this system of power, it was important to ideologically control the production of knowledge, access to schools, and popular thinking about minority groups. Cultural conflicts were a part of the American social landscape; conflicts between Protestants and Catholics, white immigrants and Native Americans, and Africans and African Americans and their white plantation owners. Native Americans, Africans, and African Americans were not supposed to attend schools or learn to read. They were told that they had no land, no history, no culture, and their Gods were heathen and 'pagan.' Through colonialism and slavery, these groups would learn about new Gods and they would go through an Americanization program to teach them how to assimilate into a new white Protestant American identity.

Since North America was a British colony, the King James Version of the Bible was the authorized text for use in church and for learning about God. The Protestant Reformation made an important departure from the authority of the Roman Catholic Church, and the Anglican Church (Church of England) became the new authorized religious denomination in all British colonies. After the Berlin conference of 1884 and the subsequent colonization of the continent of Africa (the country Ethiopia being the only exception), the Africans emerged with Bibles in their hands and images of a European savior of the world (see *Africans at the Crossroads* by John Henrik Clarke). They would also learn a new theology that suggested that the deity had chosen one select race or group of people as 'his' chosen people for most of human history, and everyone had to believe in 'his' redeemer in order to be saved. This story was a pretext for war and genocide, which was explained away through racist theology written by white supremacists. Chinua Achebe's classic novel, *Things Fall Apart,* originally published in 1959, is still one of the most widely read novels in the entire world, where he explains the impact of European colonization on the social psychology, religion, and culture of continental Africans. This novel has sold more than 11 million copies and it has been translated into more than 40 languages.

Continuing the work of de-colonization, in the late 1960s, the development of liberation theology was an important attempt to address some of the social psychological effects of group domination through repressive and hegemonic religious indoctrination that was common in slave and colonial descendents. Paulo Freire, the renowned Brazilian educator, was influenced by the movement of liberation theology, which he used in his work. Similarly, Barry Chevannes, whom I mentioned earlier in this chapter, was trained as a Jesuit priest and after travelling to the U.S. and seeing segregation and the conditions of African Americans and experiencing racial discrimination, he began to develop an understanding of the race problem in the world, something that immigrant blacks who were the majority in their home country may not have had to face directly. Chevannes also developed a great desire to understand history and African-based forms of worship in the Caribbean. Also around this time, an imposing style of popular cultural music began to emerge in Jamaica. Reggae evolved out of the natural instruments, music, sounds, and chants of the Rastafarians in the mountains of Jamaica, the most famous one being Pinnacle in Saint Catherine. The spirit and energy of this sound was later captured by the famous Bunny Lee, also known as Striker Lee, and his band

(Striker Lee, not to be confused with Lee Scratch Perry, another famous reggae producer). In Kingston, Jamaica, Bunny Lee and a group of musicians, including Glen Adams, Lester Sterling, and Bongo Herman, crafted a one-drop sound on the bass guitar with an organ shuttle and drum combination in the studio that became known as reggae, which at the time was being styled as "ghetto people's music" (Mutabaruka/Cutting Edge, 2009). People added the word "roots" before the word reggae (roots reggae) to signify that they wanted to hear the music that was socially and historically grounded. One of the popular reggae artists named Winston Rodney, otherwise known as Burning Spear, recorded a song entitled "Christopher Columbus." Spear, who was a friend of the iconic reggae singer, Robert Nesta Marley (Bob Marley), in his Columbus song he retold the history of the Caribbean from the point of view of the Arawaks and Africans who predated the Europeans' arrival in the region. Using themes from the early Caribbean researcher Joel Augustus Rogers' work, singers began to teach through their music (see Joel Rogers' *Facts about Ethiopia, Africa's Gift to the America, World's Greatest Men of Color vol. I and II*). Roots reggae was the People's University and Burning Spear was the Dean of the Institution. In this way, popular culture became one of the vehicles for decolonization. Roots reggae music was the educational and political arm of the Caribbean and later the world, which spoke to the historical and contemporary struggle for equal rights and justice. In 2010, reawakening the spirits of the ancestors, contemporary roots reggae singer Tarrus Riley, recorded a reggae thriller entitled, "Nyabinghi Pickney." In the tradition of Bob Marley and Burning Spear, in his song, Riley tells the story of the maroons in the Caribbean and freedom fighters in Africa. One of the most beloved songs on the island, Riley's tune is called, "Pickney," which is an educational track.

As mentioned, in North America, through the work of the American Colonization Society, a select number of African Americans were being afforded an education before the Civil War. Some of this was being done in part to train an overseer class who would help to govern the American colony of Liberia in West Africa. In addition, northern religious organizations aided the education of a small group of African Americans. Much of this has been documented in Carter G. Woodson's classic work, *The Education of the Negro Prior to 1861*. During this era, while the majority of blacks did not attend schools, Woodson provides an excellent account of African Americans who received an education in spite of laws that prohibited blacks from learning to read or write, or from reading anything other than the Bible. In the Reconstruction period, organizations like the Freedmen's Bureau and the

American Missionary Association began the work of developing black schools. Shortly after this, the African Methodist Episcopal Church emerged as the number one black independent institution and producer of schoolteachers. The visionary, Bishop Richard Allen, put Africa in the name of his church to reconnect African Americans to the continent of Africa and their indigenous spirituality. The progressive black church created more schools, and colleges and universities than any other black organization. James Anderson has written extensively on this in his work, *Education of Blacks in the South, 1860-1935*. In the early 20th century, Carter G. Woodson's *The Mis-Education of the Negro* chronicled the effects of European thinking and training, which was being imposed on African Americans in the name of education. Later in the 20th century, in a seminal work entitled *The College Bread Negro*, W. E. B. Du Bois explored the education and outcomes of African Americans who had obtained a college degree in the beginning of the 20th century. During the early 20th century, Atlanta University was the black Yale University and Howard University was the black Harvard. Atlanta and Howard Universities would become two of the most sought after institutions and home of some of the finest scholars. Du Bois' research and statistics on blacks in higher education would become a central resource for anyone wanting information on the topic, as it was the most definitive work at the time.

THE BOOK

This book investigates the historical developments and trends in the education and standardized testing of African Americans. It addresses the social and political dynamics of black education from 1867-1945. The book includes discussions on Booker. T. Washington, W. E. B. Du Bois, Kelly Miller, Martin Jenkins, Herman Canady, and others, in the context of black education and social progress. Much has been written on the history of education and student achievement and the challenges of providing equal educational opportunities for children in American schools. Historically, the use of intelligence testing and high stakes standardized tests as means for effecting school reform initiatives has been a sociopolitical imperative for masking structural problems in the American educational system. For too many students, the record on academic achievement reveals a legacy of failure, inadequacy and denial of educational opportunities.

This work addresses American education from the Reconstruction period to the 1940s. In doing so, it investigates educational progress during one of the most critical periods of contemporary American history.

In chapter one, I discuss the early beginnings of Atlanta University and its contributions to black education. After the Civil War, members of the American Missionary Association (AMA) founded Atlanta University (AU), the first black institution of higher learning in the state of Georgia (U.S.A.). While Bacote's (1969) *Story of the Atlanta University* presents a systematic account of the University's early beginnings, and Joseph O. Jewell's (2007) *Race, Social Reform, and the Making of a Middle Class,* provides a social class analysis on how the production of AU graduates challenged the class structure in Atlanta, few works have closely analyzed the notion of education for freedom, which was espoused by ex-slaves James Tate and Grandison B. Daniels, who founded the first black school in Atlanta, Georgia which subsequently led to the founding of AU. Furthermore, fewer works have critically examined the University's curriculum, its gendered admission practices, the intergenerational influence of its graduates, as well as the prominence of W. E. B. Du Bois at the institution. Through a critical examination of the University's programs of study and its student outcomes and testimonials, this chapter assesses the social significance of AU. It further explores the University's contributions to the social progress of African Americans and their education during and after the Reconstruction period (1867-1910). The findings reveal that the institution, and particularly its graduates, helped establish education in the South and the city of Atlanta as one of the cradles of black higher education. These findings are connected to urban education.

Connecting to the education of African Americans in the early 20th century, in chapter two, Sylvie Coulibaly explores the work of Kelly Miller and his role as a black leader and an education reformer. During the last years of the Gilded Age, as the economic and social fabric of the nation was fast changing under the rising tide of industrial capitalism, urbanization, and overseas immigration, Americans denounced the ravages of sectarian politics on the democratic system, poverty among the urban underclass, and the ills of Robber Barons. Few paid any mind to the economic and social condition of black Americans. It was during this era that a group of young black intellectuals and leaders faced the tremendous challenge of defining an agenda for racial advancement. Sociologist, columnist, and pamphleteer Kelly Miller became one of the most powerful voices in the passionate debate that ensued. While the historiography has greatly emphasized the role Booker T.

Washington and W.E.B. Du Bois played in directing racial progress for African Americans, that of Kelly Miller has been relegated to the margins. Coulibaly illustrates that between 1895 and 1915, Miller was in fact a central figure in the public and in the private debates about education for African Americans. While Kelly Miller has been wrongly labeled a straddler, he was important in articulating how all forms of education were equally valuable in achieving economic progress and full citizenship. At the turn of the 19th century, when Miller was the most widely read columnist and one of the most respected voices among black America, he used his stature to promote all educational avenues and to support a broad agenda of racial progress. Coulibaly argues that historians have mischaracterized Miller's role as that of an indecisive and minor character in light of the Washington versus Du Bois debate. Instead, Miller was adept at voicing the concerns and the needs of the black underclass while promoting racial unity among the black elite, and refusing to reduce the racial uplift to a contest between two leaders.

While Coulibaly explores the debate about education reform for African Americans, in chapter three, Cameron Seay discusses the history of racialized assessment practices in education during this time, particularly as it relates to black students and intelligence testing. Intelligence assessment has a controversial history in American education, and the controversy continues to this present day. At the core of this controversy are the assumptions that the primary factor in intelligence is heredity, and that different "races" have varying levels of intelligence. This chapter presents an analysis of the intelligence assessment literature in the first half of the twentieth century as it pertained to African Americans- then called "Negroes." A quantitative, linear, single value for human intelligence was widely accepted by American psychologists and educators. Coupled with this position was the recurring view that African Americans were measurably deficient in intelligence when compared to whites. Since the 1920s, however, there has been a substantial body of literature that has challenged both the scholarship and science of this position. An exemplary group of scholars generated voluminous and meticulous refutations to the "hereditarian" view of intelligence and its negative implications for African Americans. This chapter reviews both archived and published contributions from this body of work dating from the beginning of World War I to the end of World War II. Included are the major works of Otto Klineberg, Martin Jenkins, and Herman Canady, all of whom made substantive contributions to a "social factors" view of intellectual assessment. They and other writers made a persuasive case that it was environment, and not genetics, that was the primary force of intelligence as we know it. These findings are discussed in relation to public schools and the assessment of African Americans.

REFERENCES

Achebe, C. (1959/1994). *Things fall apart*. New York: Anchor Books.

Anderson, J. D. (1988). *The education of blacks in the south 1860-1935*. North Carolina: University of North Carolina Press.

Atkinson, L. (2006). *The earliest inhabitants: The dynamics of the Jamaican Taion*. Kingston, Jamaica: University of the West Indies Press.

Bacote, C. (1969). *The story of the Atlanta University: A century of service, 1865-1965*. Atlanta, Georgia: Atlanta University Press.

Blyden, E. (1887/1967). *Christianity, Islam and the Negro race*. Edinburg, Scotland: Edinburg University Press.

Blyden, E. W. (1908/1994). *African life and customs*. Baltimore: Black Classic Press.

Carey, B. (1997). *The Maroon story: The authentic and original history of the Maroons in the history of Jamaica, 1490-1880*. Gordon Town, Jamaica: Agouti Press.

Chevannes, B. (1994). *Rastafari roots and ideology*. Syracuse, NY: Syracuse University Press.

Clarke, J. (1991). *Africans at the crossroads: Notes for an African world revolution*. Trenton: Africa World Press, Inc.

Du Bois, W. E. B. (1910). *College-bred Negro American: Report of a social study made by Atlanta University*. Atlanta: Atlanta University Press.

James, C. L. R. (1989). *The black Jacobins: Toussaint L'Ouverture and the San Domingo revolution*. New York: Vintage Books.

James, W. (1998). *Holding aloft the banner of Ethiopia: Caribbean radicalism in early twentieth-century America*. New York: Verso.

Jewell, J. (2007). *Race, social reform and the making of the middle class: The American Missionary Association and black Atlanta 1870-1900*. Lanham, MD: Rowman and Littlefield.

Leaming, H. P. (1995). *Hidden Americans: Maroons of Virginia and the Carolinas*. New York: Garland Publishing, Inc.

Mutabaruka. (2009). Cutting edge: The history of reggae music (Live broadcast). Available at: http://www.iriefm.net/

Nettleford, R. (1970/2001). *Mirror, mirror: Identity, race and protest in Jamaica*. Kingston, Jamaica: LMH Publishing Company.

Norton, M., Sheriff, C., Katzman, D. M., Blight, D. W., Chudacoff, H., Logevall, F., and Bailey, B. (2008). *A people and a nation: A history of the United States 1492-1877* (Vol. I, 8th Edition). Boston: Houghton Mifflin.

Rogers, J. A. (1936/1982). *The real facts about Ethiopia*. Baltimore: Black Classic Press.

Rogers, J. A. (1946/1996). *World's greatest men of color Vol. I*. New York: Touchstone Book.

Rogers, J. A. (1947/1996). *World's greatest men of color Vol. II*. New York: Touchstone Book.

Rogers, J. A. (1959/1989). *Africa's gift to America*. St. Petersburg, FL.: Publisher: Helga Rogers.

Van Sertima, I. (1976). *They came before Columbus: The African presence in ancient America*. New York: Random House.

Williams, E. (1944/1994). *Capitalism and slavery*. Chapel Hill: University of North Carolina Press.

Williams, E. (1984). *From Columbus to Castro: The history of the Caribbean, 1492-1969*. New York: Vintage Books.

Williams, E. (1994). *Documents of West Indian history*. Ithaca:AB Publishing.

Woodson, C. (1919/1991). *The education of the Negro prior to 1861*. Manchester, N.H.: Ayer.

Woodson, C. (1933). *Mis-education of the Negro*. New York: AMS Press.

Chapter 1

EDUCATION FOR FREEDOM: ATLANTA UNIVERSITY AND ITS SOCIAL SIGNIFICANCE DURING AND AFTER THE RECONSTRUCTION PERIOD, 1867-1910

Greg Wiggan

I wish to thank ancestor, Asa G. Hilliard, for guidance on this project. I also wish to thank Karen L. Jefferson, archivist at the Atlanta University Center, Robert W. Woodruff Library, for her assistance and dedication to this project.

The American Missionary Association founded Atlanta University (AU) in 1867, making it the first predominately black institution of higher learning in the state of Georgia. The literature pertaining to AU addresses the institution's unique role in the progress of African Americans. For example, G. F. Richings (1969) in his book, *Evidence of Progress Among Colored People*, argues that the institution was not attempting to duplicate the educational work done by the State or most other private institutions. Rather, it was supplementing and strengthening the work of public and private schools by producing thoroughly trained individuals to carry on the education of the masses. However, few works have critically analyzed the University's curriculum, its gendered admissions practices, or the intergenerational impact of its graduates. While Clarence Bacote's (1969) *Story of the Atlanta*

University presents a systematic account of the University's early beginnings, an important work, it is more or less a house history of the institution and it provides very little critical discussion. A newer contribution is Joseph O. Jewell's (2007) *Race, Social Reform, and the Making of a Middle Class.* Jewell's work offers an intriguing discussion on how the production of AU graduates challenged the white social class structure in Atlanta.

This current research focuses less on the social class dynamics in the city of Atlanta. Instead, it examines the role that African Americans played in starting black education in Georgia (Anderson, 1988; Weber, 1978; Williams, 2005), and their belief that education was central to attaining freedom from racial domination, which connects to the founding of AU and the institution's resulting significance. While Bacote's book on the University's early development is an important work; however, questions remain such as: 1) what was the social significance of the institution and 2) how did this impact the social progress of African Americans? In this article, social significance refers to the institutional and societal impact of black higher education on the social dynamics of the broader community and its members (group level advancements and improvements). Through a critical examination of AU's programs of study, its admissions practices, its student outcomes, and the influence of W. E. B. Du Bois at the University, this research assesses the social significance of the institution on the social progress of African Americans.

Knowles Building   Boys' Hall   Stone Hall   Girls' Hall   Model Home

Atlanta University Buildings.

METHOD

This research uses archival data and records from the Special Collections Department of the Robert W. Woodruff Library in Atlanta, Georgia and other archival sources. In addition, it uses student testimonials and other primary source documents to triangulate the data. It also uses secondary sources and available graduation data in its discussion. The preponderance of this data provides a useful examination regarding the social significance of AU between 1867 and 1910.

EDUCATION FOR FREEDOM

The Reconstruction period in America was marked by the ravages of the Civil War. The war began in 1861 and ended in 1865, and within this short period of time the future of African Americans would be drastically changed (Jones, 1980, Weber, 1978). The South was devastated by the war and the pervasive task of integrating the North with the South was still at hand. The South was marked largely by a number of uneducated ex-slaves who were in many cases forced into post-slavery sharecropping, which was just as exploitative as slavery (Du Bois, 1962; Karenga, 1993). Education was needed if blacks were truly going to be free in America. In *Education of the Negro Prior to 1861*, Carter G. Woodson (1919/1991) produced a seminal work on black education during slavery. Woodson's work is pioneering, as he meticulously documents African Americans' role in education and their struggles and outcomes. African Americans' involvement in education would continue throughout the Reconstruction period.

In 1865, Congress established the Freedmen's Bureau (FB) in an attempt to address some of the challenges faced by blacks as they socialized into the new South (Du Bois, 1962; Karenga, 1993). The major duties of the FB were to guide and protect African Americans, provide medical services, help them manage their business affairs, and start black schools (Karenga, 1993). In the same year that the FB was created, black leaders established the Georgia Educational Association (GEA) to supervise and create schools, establish school policies, and raise funds for black education (Anderson, 1988; William, 2005). Black leaders knew that education was key to their freedom from second-class citizenship and for their community's progress (Weber, 1978), and the founding of the GEA was aimed at facilitating their own education. In addition to the GEA and FB education initiatives, philanthropic donations from people like George Peabody, who established the Peabody Educational Fund in 1867, John F. Slater, who founded the John Slater Fund in 1882, and people like businessman Julius Rosenwald helped to provide resources for black education in the South (Ballard, 1973). However, these philanthropic donations were often value laden and premised on vocational training and the creation of a semiskilled black worker class (Anderson & Moss, 1999).

Black church organizations like the African Methodist Episcopal Church (AME) also started their own educational institutions for blacks. After the Civil War, the AME created several church schools throughout the South, and later established black colleges and universities of higher learning for African Americans (Anderson, 1988). In addition to the AME, the American Missionary Association (AMA), a benevolent white institution, was instrumental in providing black education during the Reconstruction period. Members of the AMA founded AU, the first black school of higher education in the state of Georgia (Range, 1951; Weber, 1978). This research addresses the role that blacks played in starting black education in Georgia and its connection to the founding of AU. In addition, it critically assesses the social significance of the institution and its racial and gendered processes.

FINDINGS, BLACK EDUCATION: JAMES TATE, GRANDISON B. DANIELS, AND THE AMERICAN MISSIONARY ASSOCIATION

Around 1865 in Atlanta, Georgia, two former slaves, James Tate and Grandison B. Daniels, founded a small private school for blacks in an AME building on the corner of Courtland and Jenkins streets (AU Collection, 1800s). This was a one-room school where students ranged from ages 5-16. Although they were probably only modest teachers, the belief in education and the ideas of education for freedom and self-help were firmly established by Tate and Daniels. The duo probably learned to read from their former slave owners and they continued to teach until help arrived from northern missionaries. Despite the scarcity of information on Tate and Daniels, the two are recognized for founding Jenkins Street School, Atlanta's first school for black children (Adams, 1930; AU Collection, 1800s). During slavery, education for blacks was prohibited. While education was illegal, slave owners provided a great deal of European theology for their slaves. Slave owners understood the power of literacy and education, and they controlled access to it, making black literacy illegal and a criminal offense for slaves (Cross, 1992). A good black was one who denounced Africa, was obedient, uneducated, and was successfully cultured into plantation life and western theology. African names were forbidden, so name changes were common, and African spirituality was outlawed. Tate and Daniels knew that education had to be a top priority if the race was going to improve itself. Although Tate and Daniels have been relegated to obscurity in the discussion on black education in Georgia, they are the true pioneers.

Before the end of 1865, other sources aided black education (Jones, 1980). The AMA, headquartered in New York, was one of the northern white church institutions that sent its members to the South to teach and to create schools (Litwack, 1979). Between 1865 and 1866, among those noted AMA members who came to the South were Edmund Asa Ware, Jane Twichell – who later married Edmund Asa Ware — and Frederick and Elizabeth Ayer. The Ayers knew James Tate and Grandison B. Daniels and most likely met with them to arrange to take over the Jenkins Street School. In fact, once the AMA took over the Jenkins Street School, Tate and Daniels paid the AMA teachers and contributed money to the school's education from the meager resources they had (Rabinowitz, 1978). The Ayers, along with other AMA teachers, began to take charge of black education by teaching in whatever facilities that were available until proper school buildings could be erected (AU Collection, 1800s). The AMA would play an important role in the education of blacks in the South (Jones, 1980), and for this they were met with great resistance from Southern whites who wanted no part in racial equality or integration (Rabinowitz, 1978).

First President, Edmund Asa Ware, 1867-1885.

In 1866, Edmund A. Ware became the principal of what was now AMA's Jenkins Street School in Atlanta, while Frederick Ayer conducted the administrative and financial responsibilities of the school (Adams, 1930). The members of the AMA continued to expand the schools and increase enrollment. Ware later became the superintendent of the AMA schools in north Georgia while his colleague John A. Rockwell, who was also an AMA member, attended to the schools in southern Georgia (Adams, 1930). The AMA would later play a central role in the founding of AU.

The members of the AMA extended the vision for black education created by Tate and Daniels. This vision transcended primary and secondary schools and included higher education. In 1867, AMA members presented a charter to the Superior Court of Fulton County, petitioning for the building of a university. The petition was signed and delivered. Among the signers were Frederick Ayer, Edmund Asa Ware, and Erastus M. Cravath, who later became president of Fisk University (Adams, 1930; Bacote, 1969). Sadly, Frederick Ayer died in September of 1867, before AU opened. According to Myron Adams, fourth President of the AU, "the white people of Atlanta were glad to have Mr. Ayer die, because he was putting ideas into the heads of the colored people" (Adams, 1930, p. 8).

The charter for AU was approved in October of 1867, the same year in which it was submitted to the Fulton County Superior Court. A new corporation was formed, the Atlanta University Board of Trustees, and the next step in the establishment of the University was to secure resources for its opening. An application was filed with the Freedmen's Bureau, requesting a loan of ten thousand dollars to secure a site for the institution (Adams, 1930). After the funds were received, a site was secured and Edmund Asa Ware became the first president of the University, where he served from 1869 to 1885. After Ware died in 1885, his remains were buried on the campus of the University. Ware's remains are still on the campus, which is now Morris Brown College. In the center of the campus where Ware's burial site is marked by a large stone with a plaque on it, the following inscription is found:

> Edmund Asa Ware, First President of Atlanta University, Born in Wrentham, Massachusetts, December 22, 1837, died in Atlanta, Georgia, September 25, 1885. The graduates of Atlanta University have brought this boulder from the native town of President Ware in Massachusetts and placed it here on Georgia soil over the spot where his earthly remains lie buried in grateful memory of their former teacher and friend and of the unselfish life he lived and the noble work he wrought that their children and their children[']s children might be blessed.

The first AU building was erected in 1869, named North Hall, and the following year South Hall was erected. In 1882, an administrative building was added and named in honor of its donor, Valeria G. Stone. Stone Hall still exists today, later renamed Fountain Hall, and is located on what is now the Morris Brown College campus. Around this time, other black institutions of higher learning were being developed. Other AMA colleges and universities for blacks throughout the South included Fisk University, Straight University (later named Dillard), Talladega College, and Tougaloo College. In addition, public black colleges and universities like Florida A&M University and Alabama A&M University were created as a result of the Second Morrill Act of 1890, which provided land for the development of schools focusing on studies related to agriculture and the mechanic arts.

Another northern mission society that was instrumental in developing black institutions of higher learning was the Freedmen's Aid Society (FAS) of the Methodist Episcopal Church (Anderson, 1988; Jones, 1980). The FAS schools included: Bennett College, Clark University, Claflin College, Meharry Medical College, Morgan College, Philander Smith College, Rust College, and Wiley College. Finally, there was the leading black philanthropic organization, the African Methodist Episcopal Church. Its schools included Allen University in South Carolina, Morris Brown College in Georgia, Wilberforce College in Ohio, and Paul Quinn College in Texas, among others (Anderson, 1988; Williams, 2005). Although there were other black colleges and universities during and after the Reconstruction period, this discussion pertains to the AMA's AU.

Stone Hall Tower.

EDUCATION FOR SOCIAL PROGRESS

Atlanta University was founded in the climate of strong social opposition. Only two years after the Civil War ended, and although the majority of blacks were still uneducated, the creation of the University would be another step in the struggle to establish black education in the South. After years of working on plantation fields and being subjugated to the "anti-educationism" of slavery, blacks were not fully prepared to handle the challenges of life outside of the cotton fields (Anderson, 1973, 1988). Most grade schools for African Americans were still inadequate. Many were crammed classrooms and churches with untrained teachers who were charged with the task of educating blacks in the South. This meant that most of the graduates of these schools were not thoroughly prepared for higher learning. Consequently, many black colleges were accused of offering high school training in the name of college education (Du Bois, 1910, 1973). This criticism was pronounced against most of the attempts that were made to offer higher education to blacks, even though majority white colleges like Oberlin offered a similar type of training.

The founders of AU were aware of the criticisms charged against black higher education. In the early years after its inception, the institution offered college preparatory studies, which helped to prepare students for post-secondary training. The program provided students with three years of intense training in English, Latin, Greek, mathematics, and science. Next, there was the normal studies program, which was similar to the college preparatory program; however, it required a fourth year of training and included studies in Aesthetics and Mental and Moral Philosophies. Lastly, the most coveted studies were for those students who were admitted into the collegiate program (Du Bois, 1910).

AU did not have any collegiate graduates until 1876, the seventh year after its opening. It appears that the prior years were used to help prepare students for collegiate work. Admission into AU's collegiate program required students to pass examinations in English, algebra, geometry, history, geography, composition, Latin, and Greek (Range, 1951). Inez Viola Cantey, who was a student at AU, wrote; "When I entered Atlanta University I made the Second Normal Class" (Cantey, 1898). This statement may indicate that Cantey received an evaluation and her performance allowed her admittance into the normal studies department, rather than the collegiate department. Admission into the collegiate program was a privilege and not a right of any student.

GEORGIA'S PUBLIC EDUCATION

The expansion of public-school facilities for blacks was quite slow in Georgia. In 1871, only about 5 percent of black children were reported as attending public schools. The following year [1872], the city of Atlanta reported less than 900 black children attending public schools (Bond, 1934). Most children had to assist their parents with sharecropping so school attendance was low. Generally, the public institutions for blacks were inadequate when compared to those for whites. However, black families had a strong belief in education and they looked to mission schools like the AMA's to educate their children.

AU appeared to be one of the most sought after institutions of higher learning for blacks. The University was significant for blacks in the state of Georgia because the State made little to no provisions for black higher education, the exception being appropriations to AU (BAU, 1888b). During the 1870s, manual education in agricultural and industrial studies remained unfunded by the State. All of these studies were provided for white students, but this was not a part of the State's black education ideology. In the late 1800s, with increased social pressures and strong agitation from the African American community and from sympathetic northern whites, it became obvious to the State that it would have to provide some funding for industrial studies (meaning agricultural and manual labor) and liberal arts education. This may have been a result of the success in AU's program, and the fact that the State reluctantly acknowledged the institution's accomplishments would make this a reasonable assumption (BAU, 1888a). However, even when the State began to provide funding for industrial education, it was hardly commensurate when compared to funding for white education. When funding was offered, the State most often preferred to fund industrial, vocational education for blacks and northern philanthropists would help to provide funding where the State's resources were limited, but this was most often restricted to manual training (Cell, 1982).

In the January 1888 edition of the AU Bulletin, State contribution to black education at the University was one of the topics of discussion. The following statement was taken from that bulletin:

> For the paltry sum of $8,000 a year the State has secured for its colored youth the opportunity of all the above instruction, though costing far more than the amount of the appropriation. And all this, it has secured in an institution whose land, buildings, apparatus, library, and other equipment, it

could not duplicate for less than a quarter of a million dollars, and which have been provided for almost wholly by funds from outside the State of Georgia (BAU, 1888b).

The State was not committed to fully pursuing black higher education. It had no black institutions of higher learning of its own, and its contribution to AU's program was limited. The State's lack of interest in supporting black education might have inspired the AU's administrators and further reaffirmed the need for the institution. The University remained steadfast in its belief that the preservation of black higher education was the force to guide the destiny of black people in America.

AU's PHILOSOPHY OF EDUCATION

The belief that education was the key to black social mobility seemed to have been at the very heart of the University's administration (Jewell, 2007). The administration felt that it was producing a thoroughly educated class of young people in the South, and that self-respect, ambition, hope, courage, and progress were being transmitted to African Americans (BAU, 1894). While many of the black colleges were serving as manual labor schools, AU seemed committed to the liberal arts part of its collegiate program. Horace Mann Bond (1934) in his book, *The Education of the Negro in the American Social Order,* noted the advanced collegiate studies offered at two of the AMA schools, Fisk and Atlanta Universities. Other black schools were content with vocational studies. However, while AU had an industrial education department, it seemed to champion its cause as a liberal arts institution of higher learning for blacks.

AU's CURRICULUM

A careful examination of AU reveals a curriculum that was comprehensive both in the normal and collegiate programs. Students in the normal studies department were taught English, Latin, Mathematics, History, Bible theology, and Ethics. Other courses included Geography, Botany, Chemistry and Physics (BAU, 1883). It was the belief of President Ware and his administration that the education style found in New England colleges was desirable and should to be modeled at AU (Adams, 1930). In the normal education courses, students spent a large portion of their time studying ancient languages, sociology, and history (Du Bois, 1910). The collegiate program was even more demanding. This may have contributed to the desirability of AU college graduates. The curricular content of the collegiate program is reflected in Table 1.

Although the institution strove to offer a comprehensive program of study, it is indisputable that the training at AU was European-focused. The AMA gave birth to the institution out of its northern ideals, and students were being trained from that ideology. Courses related to pre-colonial Africa, slavery, colonialism, or the black experience were not offered and the graduates received very little in the area of their own history.

Table 1. Atlanta University's College Program Curriculum

Subjects	COURSES					
Science	Astronomy	Geology	Chemistry	Natural Philosophy		
Social Science	U.S. Const- itution	Political Economy	Science of Government	History of Civilization	Civil Liberty	Internation al Law
Religion	Natural Theology	Ethics	Evidences of Christianity	History of Reform- ation	Mental Philos- ophy Of Logic	Aesthetics
Math	Algebra	Solid and Spherical Geom- etry	Trigonom- etry	Surveying		
Language	English	Greek	Latin			

Source: Atlanta University Catalogue (1898).

In spite of the early documented record on African higher education at the University of Timbuktu in West Africa and the Grand Lodge of Luxor in Egypt, two of the first universities in the world, AU failed to incorporate any of this information into its curriculum (Bernal, 1987; Diop, 1974). Furthermore, seminal works like Edward W. Blyden's *African Problem and Other Discourses* (1890/1974), and his *African Life and Customs* (1908/1994) were never featured at AU, and there were no specific studies addressing slavery or colonialism, or issues that were affecting black people globally. Critics of this type of education argued that it was 'uncentered' and that its purpose was to socialize blacks into Western ideals. In *The Mis-Education of the Negro*, Carter G. Woodson (1933) wrote:

> The educated Negroes have the attitude of contempt toward their own
> people because in their own as well as in their mixed schools Negroes are
> taught to admire the Hebrew, the Greek, the Latin and the Teuton and to
> despise the African (p. 1).

Although Woodson wrote this in 1933, he was commenting on black
education during and after the Reconstruction period. He states:

> It may be of no importance to the race (blacks) to be able to boast today
> of many times as many educated members as it had in 1865. If they are of the
> wrong kind the increase in number will be a disadvantage rather than an
> advantage (Woodson, 1933, p. xi).

According to Woodson (1933), the wrong kinds of educated black persons
were those who had been Europeanized through their schooling. European
studies made up the core of AU's curriculum. Because of the northeastern
ideals of the University, it was not unusual to find a few graduates being
named professors of Greek in northern schools (BAU, 1885; Taylor, 1947). It
was not until the arrival of W. E. B. Du Bois in 1897 that the institution began
to make serious inquiries into black issues and the "Negro problem" (Bullock,
1967; Du Bois, 1910).

A student, Augustus Granville Dill, wrote the administration recalling his
entry into the University. He stated:

> When I came to Atlanta University I found myself very peculiarly placed
> as to classification, as I had studied neither Latin nor Greek. Dr. Adams said
> that I might begin the two languages and at the end of four weeks he would
> consider my work before giving me any other studies. I went to work with a
> will, and soon Dr. Adams added Sophomore Geometry and Second Year's
> Latin to my program (Dill, 1898).

Students like Augustus Dill were introduced to Latin and Greek studies at
AU. Regardless of which program students entered (normal or collegiate),
their studies would privilege European cultural norms and ethos. It was the
sharp criticism of black scholars on black higher education that brought about
changes in schools like AU. Du Bois and others launched strong critiques of
black education and black college curricula. In AU's collegiate program, there
was heavy emphasis on the study of Greek, Latin, and European experiences.

AU's curriculum failed to reflect any black contributions in its training.
During this time, Universities like Fisk, Atlanta, and Howard were viewed as

social settlements that imparted the culture of New England to black students. Ex-slaves were being educated to think and to behave as New Englanders. One of the outcomes of missionary education, whether intended or not, was to assimilate blacks into white cultural values and into European theology and its version of morality (McPherson, 1975). James Weldon Johnson recalls his years at AU:

> I was at the University only a short time before I began to get an insight into the ramifications of race prejudice and an understanding of the American race problem.... This knowledge was no part of classroom instruction-the college course at Atlanta University was practically the old academic course at Yale [Yale University]; the founder of the school was Edmund Asa Ware, a Yale man, and the two following presidents were graduates of Yale.. (Johnson, 1968, p. 66)

The traditional curriculum that emphasized ancient European languages would gradually change with the emergence of studies pertaining to the social conditions of black people. Educational critics like Woodson and Du Bois, whose views evolved over time, felt that higher education was beneficial, but that it was almost useless for African Americans to study from Eurocentric curricula. On the other hand, the Georgia Board of Visitors felt that blacks needed manual training, not liberal arts education, if they were going to improve their social condition (BAU, 1888a). Despite these sharp criticisms, AU continued its quest to advance higher education for blacks (Brubacher & Rudy, 1958, 1997). Moreover, before the end of the nineteen-century, Du Bois [1897] became influential when he joined the faculty at the University and began to integrate black studies into the curriculum (Anderson, 1988).

AU President Horace Bumstead asked Du Bois to join his faculty so that he could direct studies in black sociology and urbanization (McPherson, 1975). Du Bois eagerly accepted the position and continued his publications on black Americans. Du Bois' work, such as: *Philadelphia Negro* (1899), *Souls of Black Folks* (1903), *Study of the Negro Problem* (1904), and the *College-bred Negro American* (1910), quickly drew world-class attention and acclaim, and would later be considered as classics. His studies dealt with black mortality, urbanization, education, the black church, and crime. This was the first attempt in America to carry out a scientific study of the "Negro problem" (Du Bois, 1968). The AU studies of the "Negro problem," led by Du Bois, spanned from 1897-1910. These AU studies became widely distributed in libraries all over the world and were used by scholars to document works on black people. Du Bois' work helped to bring the University to new heights, as he launched studies on African Americans that had never been conducted before.

AU AND THE CREATION OF EDUCATORS

Due to the emancipation of slaves in the South, there was a great demand for schools and educators. A large portion of AU graduates joined the teaching profession where they helped to educate black children. By 1888, twenty-three of the twenty-eight (82%) black teachers in Atlanta public schools were graduates of AU, and most of the remaining five were partly trained by the University, meaning they took courses at the campus (BAU, 1888b). Between 1873 and 1894, AU's normal studies program had over 200 graduates, while the collegiate program had about 65 graduates. More than 50 percent of the graduates from the normal department pursued teaching careers and some even became professors at the collegiate level. Over 40 percent of collegiate graduates chose careers in education (AU Catalogue, 1895). The majority of these graduates worked in administrative positions or in higher education.

Normal Studies, Class of 1900.

In 1894, it was estimated that more than 15,000 children were being educated annually by graduates of AU (BAU, 1894). This was not uncharacteristic of black graduates during this time. The large production of qualified black teachers helped to create a shift in black education, gradually transitioning it back into the control and domain of the African American community. This shift from white to black teachers was gradually transforming the black educational landscape, aligning it more with the original mission of Tate and Daniels, the two ex-slaves who started the first black school in Atlanta. Although black teachers would never earn an equal pay or have equal status as their white counterparts, having competent black teachers was crucial to improving opportunities for African Americans. By 1910, more than 50 percent of all black college graduates became educators, followed by 20 percent who became preachers and pastors (Du Bois, 1910, p. 66). This trend was consistent throughout the 1920s and 1930s, where nationally the top occupations for black college graduates were teaching and the clergy (Christy & Williamson, 1992; Hill, 1985; Johnson, 1969).

GENDER AND SOCIAL CLASS AT AU

Atlanta University produced many distinguished graduates. However, most of the collegiate students were males, and although gender was not an explicit consideration for entry into the collegiate program, it may have had an influence. According to the University's catalogues, there was only one female college graduate during the institution's first 10 years of collegiate commencement ceremonies (AU Catalogue, 1895). Mary E. Badger Cummings, from the class of 1886, was the first female college graduate. In fact, the institution's records reveal that four years earlier (1882) she graduated from the normal studies department (AU Catalogue, 1895). After completing the normal studies program, she was admitted into the collegiate department where she completed her bachelor's degree and became a teacher in Galveston, Texas. It was nine years later [1895] before the University had another female graduate from its college program. In that year, there were two female graduates, Martha Freeman Childs, who became a teacher in Tuskegee, Alabama, and Georgia Louise Palmer, who taught at the Walker Institute in Augusta, Georgia (AU Catalogue, 1898). In 1896, the year following Childs and Palmer's graduation, Beatrice McGhee Curtright was the only female college graduate. Seemingly, the general low enrollment of black women in collegiate programs in the South led to the founding of Atlanta Baptist Female

Seminary [1881] in the state of Georgia, later named Spelman College (Evans, 2007). Once the school matured, businessman John D. Rockefeller became a major donor to the institution, and subsequently, it was renamed in honor of his wife Laura Spelman Rockefeller. With Rockefeller's sponsorship, Spelman College grew in prestige and admissions became more selective. By the early twentieth century, the student body became increasingly middle class, and admissions privileged students who were phenotypically, racially mixed and light complexioned.

In the early beginnings of AU, most of its female students were from Georgia and other southern states. However, as the University grew and gained national attention, it attracted students from all over the country. While female enrollment in AU's college program was less than moderate, most female students were enrolled in the normal studies department. As a result, almost all of the normal studies graduates were females, with the exception of one or two males in each graduating class. Like the collegiate graduates, most of the normal studies graduates became educators. However, the collegiate graduates were more likely to become school principals, college professors, and administrators. Although admission into the collegiate program was rigorous, one is left to speculate about why female representation was so low in the college program, while highly represented in the normal studies department. In fact, the University administration was filled with white males and white females primarily taught in the classroom. And although the female graduates from the normal studies program played an important role in increasing the number of teachers in urban and rural schools, the collegiate program was clearly a male domain. The institution may have been influenced by a social climate that was filled with female servitude. As a result, while the institution was fighting on one front against racial discrimination in education, it may have been overlooking the intersection of race and gender discrimination. Most of the collegiate educational needs of black women would be attended to by the neighboring school, Spelman College (Cross, 1992).

Other black women colleges formed as black women's education grew, where Bennett College [1873] in Greensboro, North Carolina and Hartshorn Memorial College for women in Richmond, Virginia [1883] also helped produce graduates. Similarly, in *Black Women in the Ivory Tower*, Stephanie Evans (2007) illustrates the struggles of black women in the academy and the emergence of black women collegiate graduates. Evans (2007) argues compellingly that black women encountered additional structural barriers and discriminations that made access to collegiate education exceptionally difficulty, and she chronicles their attendance and graduation rates. However, by the 1920s, black females would nationally outpace their male counterparts in collegiate completion rates (Johnson, 1969). Much of this could be attributed to gradual changes in gender roles and an increase in the number of institutions educating women.

With the growing number of prominent graduates from AU, the school was gaining the status of an elite black institution. Although the students' social class cannot be easily determined, it does appear that by the late 1800s the University began to appeal to students from an upper-middle class. In its formative years, most of its students were children of ex-slaves who were primarily from the state of Georgia. However, by the early 1900s the University attracted students from all over the United States (BAU, 1938).

AU GRADUATES

Although the majority of AU graduates were from the normal school, this next section emphasizes the institution's collegiate graduates because black college graduates were rare during this time (1867-1910), and although the graduating classes were small, they were all well accomplished (Mather, 1915). In each of its graduating class, AU gave birth to new leaders in the black social order. While mentioning all of the graduating classes is beyond the scope of this chapter, in covering most of the early classes, the intent is to illustrate the impact of the University and its graduates. In the class of 1876, which was the first collegiate class to graduate from the University, there were several notable individuals. William Henry Crogman graduated from this class, and he became a distinguished Professor of Ancient Languages at Clark University in Georgia. He also served as president of Clark University from 1903-1910, making him the institution's first black president (National Freedom Day Association, 2000; Towns, 1934).

Other members of the graduating class of 1876 were Reverend Edgar Penny who became a teacher, minister, and chaplain at Tuskegee Institute. In addition, Samuel B. Morse and London H. Waters were members of this class, and they both became outstanding educators (Bacote, 1969). Richard R. Wright was a member of this class as well. Wright became president of Georgia State College, president of the Georgia Colored Fair Association, president of the Georgia Agricultural and Industrial Association, president of the National Association of Teachers in Colored Schools, and president of the National Negro Bankers Association (BAU, 1938; Hartshorn & Penniman,

1910). The following year [1877], John McIntosh graduated and became a teacher in Savannah, Georgia. He also held a position as a state legislature, in which he represented Liberty County in the Georgia House of Representatives (Bacote, 1969).

William H. Crogman.

In the class of 1879, there were two notable graduates, John L. Dart and Edwin Posey Johnson. After graduating from AU, Dart became a public school teacher and then a Baptist pastor. He later founded Charleston Normal and Industrial Institute for blacks (Pegues, 1892). In addition, Edwin Johnson became an instructor in the Divinity Department of Morehouse College and was a Baptist pastor (Richardson, 1919).

In 1881, Paul Edward Spratlin graduated from AU. Later he continued his education and received his Medical Doctorate from Denver Medical College in Colorado. Spratlin practiced medicine in Denver and later became chief medical inspector for the state. Also, in this class were Preston Peters and Butler Wilson. Peters was a principal in Columbus, Georgia and an ordained minister (Gaines, 1890). Butler Wilson was a prominent lawyer in Boston and a financial supporter of AU. In Boston, Wilson built a lucrative law firm and was appointed Master of Chancery of the courts (Bacote, 1969).

In 1882, Oswell Augustus Combs graduated from AU. Combs became a Professor of Greek and Latin and a music teacher. He was awarded three premiums and a silver medal and was twice appointed teacher of penmanship in the Peabody Normal Institute. Later, he was chosen to be the chair of Greek and International Law at Allen University in Columbia, South Carolina (Caldwell, 1917). Henry Walker graduated in the same class as Combs. Walker was Principal of Ware High School in Augusta, Georgia, and was the first black educator in the state to be regularly employed as an expert for the Peabody Institute (Bacote, 1969).

Richard R. Wright 1876.

Loring B. Palmer graduated in the class of 1891, and he taught in Georgia State College at Savannah. He later received his Medical Doctorate from the University of Pennsylvania and then became president of the Tri-State Medical Association of Florida, Georgia, and Alabama (Kenney, 1912). In addition, Julius Styles graduated from this class as well. Styles was an educator and a social activist, and he was named delegate for Georgia to attend several Republican National Conventions (Caldwell, 1917).

The class of 1894 was equally impressive as the other graduating classes. Among these distinguished graduates were James Weldon Johnson and George Towns. While at AU, the duo took first and third place prizes for composition and oratory in competitions arranged by the Quiz Club of Boston (BAU, 1892; Bumstead, 1895). Both of these graduates became school principals and community activists. Johnson became renowned as a scholar, activist, songwriter, and founder of the newspaper, *The Daily American*. Johnson wrote the famous "Negro National Anthem" and he made history in Florida, being the very first black person to pass the Florida Bar Examination (Johnson, 1968).

George A. Towns.

Benjamin Allen was also in the same graduating class as Johnson and Towns, and upon graduating, he became professor of ancient languages at Lincoln University (Bumstead, 1895). The success of AU and its graduates challenged the racial inferiority claims that were being legitimated by racist university researchers. These beliefs were prevalent in the South, across the nation and around the world (Jewell, 2007; Wiggan, 2007).

Classes, 1894.

AU RECEIVES RECOGNITION AND CRITICISM: DID RACE REALLY MATTER?

Through the success of its graduates, AU's social significance in the progress of African Americans was recognized. Clarence Bacote quotes General Samuel C. Armstrong, President of the Hampton Institute, who favored manual education for blacks, as praising the work of AU and stating that it was preeminently fitted to become a great university (Bacote, 1969). By 1910, AU was ranked as a first-rate college and was named among the eight institutions with the largest number of black college graduates (Du Bois, 1910, 1973). The universities that achieved this level of distinction required 14 or more units of entrance requirements and had more than 20 students of college rank. This same standard was used to rank white colleges and universities. The number of college units required for entry by AU was even higher than some white institutions. The University of Georgia, then the University of Athens, required 12 units, and the University of Virginia required 11.5, while AU required 14 (Du Bois, 1910). Although there were other black institutions of higher learning being created in Georgia, like Clark University [1877], [1] Atlanta Baptist Seminary/Morehouse College[2] [1879], Spelman, and Morris Brown Colleges [1881], they had not yet risen to the status of their precursor, AU. A prominent Georgia politician, Representative W. C. Glenn, stated, "It (AU) was the best Institution of the kind in Georgia" (BAU, 1888c). Even the members of the State Board of Visitors commented on the quality of AU's college program. Below are some of the Board members' comments that were taken from an interview by the Augusta Chronicle, which were republished in the University's bulletin.

- At every step of the examination we were impressed with the fallacy of the popular idea (which in common with thousands of others, a majority of the undersigned have heretofore entertained) that the members of the African race are not capable of a high grade of intellectual culture. The rigid tests to which the classes in Algebra and Geometry and in Latin and Greek, were subjected unequivocally demonstrated that under judicious training, and with persevering study, there are many members of the African race who can attain a high grade of intellectual culture..... Many of the pupils exhibited a degree of mental culture, which considering the length of time their minds have been in training would do credit to members of any race. (BAU, 1888c, pp. 2-3)
- There is not a white school or college in the State that is so well equipped as the Atlanta University; that has a faculty of such thorough teachers; an attendance so well disciplined; or buildings and apparatus so perfect in detail. (BAU, 1888c, p. 5)
- Do you know, there are seven white pupils in the same school, and that they occupy desks in the same rooms, sit on the same recitation benches with the colored pupils, and are shown no difference? Six of them are children of members of the faculty. (BAU, 1888c, p. 7)
- I believe white children would do just as well if they had the same advantages those Negro children have. (BAU, 1888c, p.7)

---

[1]Clark's primary school was opened in 1869 by Reverend W. Lee, and it was chartered as a university in 1877.
[2]The Atlanta Baptist Seminary was born out of the Augusta Institute of 1867, and was charted in 1879. In 1913, the name was changed to Morehouse College in honor of Henry Lyman Morehouse.

Even with these strong reviews of AU's program, the Board of Visitors discouraged further use of any State funds to support black higher education (BAU, 1888c). Board president, Joseph E. Brown, a former slave owner and Georgia Confederate governor, "made it clear that black education would facilitate Southern whites taking 'a friendly control of the colored population'" (Jewell, 2007, p. 92). As Brown indicates, the State was only interested in black education that would allow whites to maintain their control of - and privilege over blacks. The Board regarded State support of black higher education not only as intrinsically wrong, but also as an improper use of money appropriated by the State. What is intriguing is that the State Board of Visitors never criticized AU for not offering a quality education to students. Rather, they repeatedly praised that part of the work (BAU, 1888c). However, the culture in the South was still anti-black and racist, and the idea of social equality was still an illusion.

A rather dubious explanation was given by the State as its reason for revoking appropriations to AU. In response to the minority of white students who were attending AU, mostly children of the faculty, as was reported by one of the visitors from the Board, the State decided to reform its appropriations. It was expressed that the State and the people of Georgia declared their unalterable opposition to the integration of the races in schools (BAU, 1888c). Georgia Representative W. C. Glenn was quoted as stating that revoking the appropriation was a punishment for teaching white and colored children in the same institution (BAU, 1888c). While there were only a few white students at the University, the State found it objectionable for any white student to be in the same institution with black students. The South struggled with the issue of interracial classrooms and AU was caught in the segregationist politics of the State. Although the Civil Rights Act of 1875 aimed to secure more rights for blacks, most Southern whites upheld lynching, segregation, and racial exclusion (Rabinowitz, 1978). The AMA and other northern missionaries posed a threat to the racialized social class system of the South, and Southern whites did not appreciate it (Jewell, 2007).

The AU administrators had to have known the State's position on coeducation of the races because the State Board of Visitors had been visiting the institution since 1871, and must have given them guidelines for retaining State support. The State Board of Visitors had no commitment to integration. However, "many of the teachers (AU) came with the hope of teaching whites and blacks in the same schools. As a representative of the AMA later said..." (Rabinowitz, 1978, p. 154). It seems clear that the AU administrators were unwilling to discriminate against persons of any race who wanted to enroll in the institution. Although the State funds were hardly sufficient, the decision by the State would remove a significant part of the University's budget. Despite this disappointment, the AU administration continued its mission. Its purpose was well established, and blacks seemed to cherish the cause of this social institution of progress.

In sum, AU was created at a crucial time in the history of African Americans. The Civil War had ended and slaves were freed. However, their lack of education and their race made them a lower class of people. Education was needed for black social progress. Through the vision of James Tate and Grandison B. Daniels who created the first school for blacks in Atlanta, Jenkins Street School, the AMA members who took over the school, became instrumental in building on that legacy of providing education for blacks. Later, AU made it possible for African Americans to receive higher education, and it created new opportunities for future generations. Myron Adams served at AU from 1889-1929 and was named acting president in 1923 during the illness of President Bumstead. When commenting on the institution, Adams wrote: "The glory of the Atlanta University has been in the life of those who have received its training" (Adams, 1930, p. 20). The success of the University was almost unquestionable. Although unwilling to give full support, the state of Georgia praised the University for its accomplishments.

During the Presidency of Horace Bumstead (1888-1907), a graduate, Mary Hubert, writes the institution with great joy as she extolled the administration on how her education at the University impacted her life. She wrote:

> Though busy in the classroom, I have not forgotten to send up my prayers for the prosperity of Atlanta University. I really love the school and the faithful and earnest teachers connected with it.... I was offered the position of principal of a school about thirty miles from home. Being a graduate of the Atlanta University, I could have accepted an appointment in a city public school (Hubert, 1898).

Mary Hubert's testimonial revealed how her life was touched by AU. The word "love" was used to describe her feelings for the institution. She mentioned that being an AU graduate, she was offered a principal job in the city, evidently one of the most sought after locations at the time. However, Hubert decided to accept an offer in the country where she could possibly make a greater contribution.

By the late eighteen hundreds, the institution reached a great level of prominence and was recognized for its academic excellence. The University had become a fortress of hope: a cradle of change, a social force in black education and it was revolutionary in its philosophy that higher education and social progress for African Americans were inseparable. In 1889, the institution received a Silver Medal at the Piedmont Exposition in Atlanta (BAU, 1889). With the arrival of the scholar W.E. B. Du Bois in 1897, AU reached national acclaim (Lewis, 1993, 2000). *The New York Tribune* hailed Du Bois and AU for their work in the progress of black Americans and for the Paris Negro Exhibit from the University (Lewis, 1993, 2000; New York Tribune, 1900).

Later, there was a heated debate between Du Bois and Booker T. Washington over the type of education that was best suited for black students. Due to Washington's association and recognition among white philanthropic organizations, which favored industrial education, Du Bois' opposition to Washington placed AU, a liberal arts institution, in the spotlight, making it difficult for the institution to secure funding for its general program (Lewis, 1993, 2000). Throughout the South, white philanthropic donations played a key role in the establishment of black education, but they often did so with the intent of creating a new class of manual laborers who were submissive (Anderson & Moss, 1999). While Southern whites feared that educated blacks would challenge the white establishment, philanthropists like Julius Rosenwald saw manual training and Booker T. Washington style politics as best suited for African Americans (Anderson & Moss, 1999).

Due to AU's growing need for philanthropic donations, Du Bois' open criticisms regarding the limitations of vocational training, which was often prescribed by external donors, posed a problem (Du Bois, 1973; Lewis, 1993, 2000). The administration was forced to reconsider retaining him on its faculty. AMA's external funding needs were a priority (McPherson, 1975). Because of the oppositional climate faced by Du Bois, in 1910 he resigned and accepted an offer from the National Association for the Advancement of Colored People in New York, of which he helped to incorporate. By then, Du Bois' contributions to the University were already made and the institution was well-renowned (Lewis, 1993, 2000).

According to Allen B. Ballard (1973) in his book, *The Education of Black Folk*, by the 1900s, AU became one of the shelters for black scholars. Although the institution was far from perfect, often overlooking the intersection of race and gender, while teaching from a curriculum that emphasized white cultural ethos and seemly attempting to silence Du Bois, its most acclaimed researcher and faculty member, Ballard was insightful in calling the institution a shelter because it acted as a refuge for African Americans desiring an education for the social progress of their race. The implications of AU are important for a better understanding of black resiliency in education, and self-determination through the founding work of ex-slaves Tate and Daniels, who founded the first school for black children in Atlanta, Jenkins Street School, which later led to the creation of AU. Later, Du Bois' pioneering work in the *Philadelphia Negro* (1899) — the first work in urban sociology — as well as his studies at AU on the "Negro problem" and education, helped establish the crucial intersection of urban education and urban sociology as a modern field of study.

REFERENCES

Adams, M. W. (1930). *The history of the Atlanta University*. Atlanta: Atlanta University Press.

Anderson, J. D. (1973). *Education for servitude: The social purpose of the schooling in the black south*. Doctoral dissertation, University of Illinois, Urbana-Champaign.

Anderson, J. D. (1988). *The education of blacks in the south 1860-1935*. North Carolina: University of North Carolina Press.

Anderson, E., and Moss, A., Jr. (1999). *Dangerous donations: Northern philanthropy and southern black education, 1902-1930*. Columbia: University of Missouri Press.

AU Collection. (1800s). Beginnings of education among the freedmen in Atlanta. *Atlanta University Collection 87-007-03. 001*. Atlanta, Georgia: Robert W. Woodruff Library Archives.

AU Catalogue. (1895). *AU catalogue of the officers and students of Atlanta University* (G.F., Foote and Davies Company). Atlanta, Georgia: Robert W. Woodruff Library Archives.

AU Catalogue. (1898). *AU catalogue of the officers and students of Atlanta University*. (G.F., Foote and Davies Company). Atlanta, Georgia: Robert W. Woodruff Library Archives.

Bacote, C. (1969). *The story of the Atlanta University: A century of service, 1865-1965*. Atlanta, Georgia: Atlanta University.

Ballard, A. B. (1973). *The education of black folk: The Afro-American struggle for knowledge in white America*. New York: Harper and Row.

BAU. (1883, November). Grammar and normal departments. *Bulletin of Atlanta University No. 1.* Atlanta, Georgia: Atlanta University Press, Robert W. Woodruff Library Archive.

BAU. (1885, November). T. Chase, odds and ends. *Bulletin of Atlanta University No. 2.* Atlanta, Georgia: Atlanta University Press, Robert W. Woodruff Library Archives.

BAU. (1888a, November). A symposium. *Bulletin of Atlanta University No. 4.* Atlanta, Georgia: Atlanta University Press, Robert W. Woodruff Library Archives.

BAU. (1888b, January). What Atlanta University has done for Georgia. *Bulletin of Atlanta University No. 4.* Atlanta, Georgia: Atlanta University Press, Robert W. Woodruff Library Archives.

BAU. (1888c, November). Our appeal. *Bulletin of Atlanta University No. 4.* Atlanta, Georgia: Atlanta University Press, Robert W. Woodruff Library Archives.

BAU. (1889, November). Silver medal received at the Piedmont Exposition. *Bulletin of Atlanta University No. 13.* Atlanta, Georgia: Atlanta University Press, Robert W. Woodruff Library Archives.

BAU. (1892, June). Quiz club prizes. *Bulletin of Atlanta University No. 38.* Atlanta, Georgia: Atlanta University Press, Robert W. Woodruff Library Archives.

BAU. (1894, October). General statement for 1894-95 (26th year). *Bulletin of Atlanta University No. 58.* Atlanta, Georgia: Atlanta University Press, Robert W. Woodruff Library Archives.

BAU. (1938, December). Richard R. Wright: Atlanta University's oldest living college graduate. *Bulletin of Atlanta University No. 24.* Atlanta, Georgia: Atlanta University Press, Robert W. Woodruff Library Archives.

Bernal, M. (1987). Black *Athena: The Afroasiatic roots of classical civilization* [volume 1]. New Brunswick: Rutgers University Press.

Blyden, E. W. (1890/1974). *African problem and other discourses.* London: W. B. Whittingham and Company.

Blyden, E. W. (1908/1994). *African life and customs. Baltimore*: Black Classic Press.

Bond, H. M. (1934). The education of the Negro in the American social order. NY: Prentice-Hall.

Brubacher, J. S., and Rudy, W. (1958). *Higher education in transition: An American history* 1636-1956 (1st ed.). New York: Harper and Brother.

Brubacher, J. S, and Rudy, W. (1997*). Higher education in transition: A history of American colleges and universities* (4th ed.). New Brunswick: New Jersey Transaction Publisher.

Bullock, H. A. (1967). *A history of Negro education in the south: From 1619 to the present.* Cambridge, Massachusetts: Harvard University Press.

Bumstead, H. (1895, November). What the college graduates of the Atlanta University are doing. Bulletin of Atlanta University No. 61 (Horace Bumstead Records B23:F4). Atlanta, Georgia: Atlanta University Press, Robert W. Woodruff Library Archives.

Caldwell, A. B. (Ed.). (1917). *History of the American Negro and his institutions.* Atlanta: A. B. Caldwell Publishing Company, GA Edition.

Cantey, I. V. (1898). Letter to Atlanta University: Horace Bumstead President, M.W. Adams Treasurer, and Miss Frances B. Clemmer, Local Secretary (1898-1904). *Presidential Records Box 20 Folder 1.* Atlanta, Georgia: Robert W. Woodruff Library Archives.

Cell, J. W. (1982). *The highest stage of white supremacy: The origins of segregation in South Africa and the American South.* New York: Cambridge University Press.

Christy, R. D., and Williamson, L. (Eds.) (1992). *A century of service: Land-grant colleges and universities, 1890-1990.* New Brunswick: New Jersey Transaction Publisher.

Cross Brazzell, J. (1992, January/February). Bricks without straw: Missionary-sponsored black higher education in the post-emancipation era. *Journal of Higher Education*, 63(1), 26-49.

Dill, A. G. (1898). Letter to the Atlanta University: Horace Bumstead President, M.W. Adams Treasurer, and Miss Frances B. Clemmer, Local Secretary (1898-1904). *Presidential Records Box.* 20, Folder 1. Atlanta, Georgia: Robert W. Woodruff Library Archive.

Diop, C. (1974). *The African origin of civilization: Myth or reality* (M. Cook, Trans.). Chicago: Lawrence Hill Books.

Du Bois, W. E. B. (1899). *The Philadelphia Negro: A social study.* Philadelphia: University of Pennsylvania.

Du Bois, W. E. B. (1903). *Souls of black folks.* New York: Bantam.

Du Bois, W. E. B. (1904). *The study of the Negro problem.* Atlanta: Atlanta University Press, Robert W. Woodruff Library Archive.

Du Bois, W. E. B. (1910). *College-bred Negro American: Report of a social study made by Atlanta University.* Atlanta: Atlanta University Press.

Du Bois, W. E. B. (1962). *Black reconstruction in America: An essay toward a history of the part which black folk played in the attempt to reconstruct democracy in America 1860-1880*. Cleveland: World Publication Company.

Du Bois, W. E. B. (1968). *The autobiography of W. E. B. Du Bois: A soliloquy on viewing my life from the last decade of this first century*. New York: International Publishers.

Du Bois, W. E. B. (1973). *The education of black people*. New York: Antehneum.

Evans, S. Y. (2007). *Black women in the ivory tower, 1850-1954: An intellectual history*. Gainesville: University Press of Florida.

Gaines, W. (1890). *African Methodism in the south: Twenty-five years of freedom*. Atlanta, Georgia: Franklin Publishing House.

Hartshorn, W. N., and Penniman, G. W. (Eds.). (1910). *An era of progress and promise 1863-1910*. Boston, Massachusetts: Priscilla Publishing Company.

Hill, S. T. (1985). *The traditionally black institutions of higher education 1860-1982*. Washington, DC: National Center for Education Statistics.

Hubert, M. L. (1898). Letter to the Atlanta University: Horace Bumstead President, M.W. Adams Treasurer, and Miss Frances B. Clemmer, Local Secretary (1898-1904). *Presidential Records Box 20*. Atlanta, Georgia: Robert W. Woodruff Library Archives.

Jewell, J. (2007). *Race, social reform and the making of the middle class: The American Missionary Association and black Atlanta 1870-1900*. Lanham, MD: Rowman and Little field.

Johnson, C. S. (1969). *The Negro college graduate*. New York: Negro Universities Press.

Johnson, J. W. (1968). *Along this way: The autobiography of James Weldon Johnson*. New York: Viking Press. (Original work published 1933)

Jones, J. (1980) *Soldiers of light and love: Northern teachers and Georgia blacks, 1865-1873*. Chapel Hill: University of North Carolina Press

Karenga, M. (1993*). Introduction to black studies*. Los Angles, California: University of Sankore Press.

Kenney, J. (1912). *The Negro in medicine*. Tuskegee Institute, Alabama: Tuskegee Institute Press.

Lewis, D. L. W.E.B. (1993). *W. E. B. Du Bois: Biography of a race, 1868-1919*. New York: H. Holt.

Lewis, D. L. (2000). *W. E .B. Du Bois: The fight for equality and the American century 1919-1963*. New York: H. Holt.

Litwack, L. F. (1979). *Been in the storm so long: The aftermath of slavery*. New York: Alfred A. Knopf.

Mather, F. L. (Ed.). (1915). *Who's who of the colored race Vol. I.* Chicago, Illinois: Memento Edition.

McPherson, J. M. (1975). *The abolitionist legacy: From reconstruction to the NAACP.* Princeton: Princeton University Press.

National Freedom Day Association. (2000). *Life and times of major Richard Robert Wright, Sr. biographical files.* Atlanta: Robert W. Woodruff Library Archives.

New York Tribune. (1900, April, 29). Progress of the Negro: An exhibit for the Paris Exposition, which illustrates it (Horace Bumstead Records: B23: F6). Atlanta, Georgia. Robert W. Woodruff Library Archives.

Pegues, A. W. (1892). *Our Baptist ministers and schools.* Springfield, Massachusetts: Willey and Company.

Perry, T. Steele, C., and Hilliard, A. III. (2003). *Young, gifted, and black: Promoting high achievement among African-American students.* Boston: Beacon Press.

Rabinowitz, H. (1978). *Race relations in the urban south 1865-1890.* New York: Oxford University Press.

Range, W. (1951). *The rise and progress of Negro colleges in Georgia 1865-1949.* Athens, Georgia: University of Georgia Press.

Richardson, C. (Ed.). (1919). *The national cyclopedia of the colored race Vol. 1.* Jefferson City, Missouri: National Publishing Company.

Richings, G. F. (1969). *Evidence of progress among colored people.* Chicago: Afro-Am Press.

Taylor, I. E. (1947). Negro teachers in white colleges. *School and Society,* 65, 370-372.

Towns, G. (1934, April). William Henry Crogman. *Journal of Negro History,* 19, 213.

Weber, T. L. (1978). *Deep like the rivers: Education in the slave quarter communities, 1831-1865.* New York: W. W. Norton.

Wiggan, G. (2007). Race, school achievement and educational inequality: Towards a student-based inquiry perspective. *Review of Educational Research,* 77(3), 310-333.

Williams, H. A. (2005). *Self-taught: African American education in slavery and freedom: 1861-1871.* Chapel Hill: University of North Carolina.

Woodson, C. G. (1919/1991). *The education of the Negro prior to 1861.* Manchester, N.H.: Ayer. (Original work published 1919)

Woodson, C. G. (1933). *The mis-education of the Negro.* Trenton, New Jersey: Associated Press.

Chapter 2

STRADDLER NO MORE: KELLY MILLER AND THE FIGHT OVER BLACK EDUCATION IN THE AGE OF BOOKER T. WASHINGTON, 1895-1915

Sylvie Coulibaly

The historical narrative that chronicles black intellectual life from the end of the Gilded Age to World War I is well known. In the early 1960s, August Meier's works, "The Racial and Educational Philosophy of Kelly Miller, 1895-1915" (1960) and especially *Negro Thought in Black America, 1880-1915: Racial Ideologies in the Age of Booker T. Washington* (1964), painted a portrait of an intelligentsia profoundly divided by their views on, and methods for, achieving full black citizenship and equality. Meier asserted that the seminal moment in the period was Booker T. Washington's 1895 Atlanta Exposition address. Meier argued that when Washington told African Americans to "cast down" their buckets with the whites of the South, he compromised full political rights and the end of Jim Crow segregation in favor of economic uplift. Meier added that in Washington's plan for industrial education and his desire to secure the financial backing of white philanthropists, the former slave sacrificed the right of blacks to higher education. Meier concluded that for the next twenty years Washington, backed by moderate whites, became the *de facto* master of much of black America, while W.E.B. Du Bois emerged and rose to prominence as a militant champion of black equality and Washington's principal opponent.

From the 1960s through the 1980s, historians have framed their analyses of black intellectual discourse in the Age of Jim Crow using Meier's Washington-Du Bois dichotomy. While there is little doubt that these two men wielded tremendous influence over African American affairs, they did not encapsulate the totality of the black intellectual experience. Beginning in the mid-1980s, a few historians began to recognize this complexity. Louis Harlan's two-volume biography of Booker T. Washington, *Booker T. Washington: The Making of a Black Leader* (1975) and *Booker T. Washington: The Wizard of Tuskegee, 1901-1915*, (1986) revealed Washington's desire for racial equality and his clandestine efforts to ameliorate segregation. James Anderson's (1988) *The Education of Blacks in the South, 1860-1935*, also presented a more balanced account of black intellectual life. Despite these revisionist efforts, historians of the black intellectual tradition have largely continued to use the Washington versus Du Bois, Conservatives versus Radicals, and industrial education versus liberal arts schema.

In this chapter, I argue that the dichotomy centered on Washington and Du Bois is a reductive and incomplete understanding of black intellectual life between the end of the Gilded Age and World War I. Both Washington and Du Bois believed in education according to opportunity, that is, that students with sufficient talent and the inclination should pursue a liberal arts education, while those without such abilities and proclivities should be trained in the industrial arts. Despite having this sensible, balanced view of education for African Americans, outside forces compelled each man to most stridently advocate for the position with which he was most closely associated, liberal arts education for Du Bois and industrial education for Washington. White educational philanthropists were largely responsible for forcing the two men into these antagonistic positions. White backers favored Washington and his industrial arts program over the liberal arts, thus enhancing Washington's power but potentially damaging liberal arts institutions. Du Bois saw this threat and felt compelled to combat it, thus putting him on a collision course with Washington. Rather than risk the loss of white philanthropic support—and all that he had worked a lifetime for—Washington felt that he had no choice but to silence Du Bois and his allies. The strife between these two educational giants created a division that came to define the discourse surrounding black educational empowerment, but one that did not represent the thinking or desires of most blacks on the issue.

I illustrate that Kelly Miller—an underappreciated and understudied black thinker—was a central figure in the debate over education and civil rights. He was representative of most black intellectuals who did not believe that racial uplift was either conservative or liberal but both, depending on circumstances. From the 1880s to his death in 1939, Miller was one of the most prominent voices among the black intelligentsia. A columnist syndicated in hundreds of newspapers, including the *Washington Post*, an extremely productive writer and renowned essayist, Miller was front and center in all the debates that engaged the black world. Unlike what August Meier, Jonathan Scott Holloway, William Banks, Louis Harlan, Willard B. Gatewood, and David L. Lewis have argued, Miller was not a "straddler," one who was incapable of making up his mind or of choosing between Washington and Du Bois (Banks, 1999; Gatewood, 1990; Holloway, 2002; Lewis, 1993; Meier, 1960). I argue that Kelly Miller knowingly rejected that either/or proposition. Instead, he was a pragmatist who believed that in order to maximize their opportunities for racial advancement, African Americans should utilize all their strengths and employ all relevant strategies from whatever source, as long as they produced results. His position was not marginal, but instead represented the approach adopted by most black intellectuals and leaders; they valued both Washington's and Du Bois' agendas and methods. Miller does not deserve the pejorative label "straddler" with which he has been branded; he was a flexible thinker who understood that while the liberal arts of the Talented Tenth had to play a central role in the race's advancement, industrial education was no less essential for achieving full citizenship. Miller also knew that the backing of moderate influential whites and the political, economic, and racial realities of the era could not be ignored or opposed on principle alone. Because he was not held in the thrall of white educational philanthropic interests or considered by Washington an implacable foe, Miller could articulate a view of black education that Washington and Du Bois would have shared, but that they could not publicly defend with alacrity. Miller became the champion of education based on opportunity, the position held by most black leaders.

THE FOUNDATIONS OF KELLY MILLER'S EDUCATIONAL VISION

Kelly Miller was born in the middle of the Civil War, on the same fateful day, July 18, 1863, that the all-black 54th Massachusetts Volunteer Infantry

Regiment launched its heralded but ill-fated assault on Fort Wagner in South Carolina. Born in neighboring Winnsboro to a slave mother and a free black father, Kelly Miller would transcend his very humble beginnings to become one of the most successful and acclaimed black academics and leaders of his time. Miller's journey from picking cotton on his parents' farm in Fairfield County to becoming a premier sociologist, academic, essayist, columnist, and commentator on the condition of African Americans would span almost fifty years. From Howard University, his alma mater and intellectual stronghold, Miller was in the vanguard of the fights for black education, civil rights and full-citizenship, economic advancement, and combating racism at home and abroad. By the 1920s, Miller was a sociology professor who traveled extensively—often at his own expense—to address black and white audiences. He was also a prolific author who wrote pamphlets and essays that circulated widely among African Americans, making him "perhaps the most successful of his race" at reaching the masses through literature (Eisenberg, 1960, p. 182). More than 100,000 readers read his open letters to Thomas Dixon and to President Warren G. Harding. Eisenberg writes that "It was said in 1923 that, 'No journalist today speaks weekly to a larger mass of colored Americans than Dean Kelly Miller of Howard University" (Eisenberg, 1960, p. 183). In 1937, H. L. Mencken praised Miller, saying that he was "amazed' and "delighted" by his writings. Miller was regularly dubbed "the Negro's chief intellectual protagonist" (Eisenberg, 1960, p. 182). However, today Miller is all but forgotten. It is largely because he would not take sides in the partisan educational debate between Booker T. Washington and W.E.B. Du Bois.

Addressing a crowd of mostly white Southerners at the Atlanta Cotton States Exposition in 1895, Booker T. Washington tried to woo hostile or incredulous white listeners by assuring them that racial uplift for blacks only meant economic, not social, progress. Toward that end, Washington famously exhorted African Americans to "Cast down your buckets where you are," to remain in the South, cooperate with white southerners, and to lift their race through hard work (Washington, 1919, p. 219). In urging this course of action, Washington set the stage for a titanic intellectual clash and Kelly Miller would find himself right in the middle of it.

The initial reaction to Washington's address was mixed. Some black intellectuals, including Du Bois, Washington's staunchest future rival, thought the speech was an excellent bit of statecraft, a workable solution to the vexing problem of how blacks could advance in a hostile South. On September 24th, 1895, while teaching at Wilberforce University, W.E.B. Du Bois wrote to Washington, "Let me heartily congratulate you on your phenomenal success at

Atlanta-it was a word fitly spoken" (Harlan, 1975, p. 26). Similarly effusive in his praise was T. Thomas Fortune in a letter that reached Washington the day after Du Bois': "It looks as if you are our [Frederick] Douglass, the best equipped of the lot of us to be the single figure ahead of the procession" (Harlan, 1975, p. 31). Like Du Bois and Fortune, many black leaders were pleased that a black man had been given such a prominent role at a white southern affair, and that he had struck a compromise without demeaning the race in the process.

Not all black leaders were so sanguine, however. Some were convinced that Washington had told the white world that blacks no longer desired social and political equality, and as part of that abject surrender, had also agreed to renounce blacks' desire for liberal arts education. Black intellectuals who believed that higher learning should remain an option for the brightest African Americans decided to take action. On the evening of December 18, 1896, at the invitation of Alexander Crummell, Kelly Miller met with Paul Laurence Dunbar and Walter B. Hayson at the Washington D.C. residence of lawyer and editor of the *People's Advocate* John Wesley Cromwell. The meeting's purpose was to discuss the birth of a literary society. The American Negro Academy was the result of years of intense debate among black leaders, among them Frederick Douglass and Edward Wilmot Blyden, as to whether racial uplift should rest upon liberal arts or industrial education. Booker T. Washington's Atlanta address became the catalyst for Crummell's decision to create the academy. On March 1897, Crummell's dream of creating an organization of "authors, scholars, artists…of African descent" finally became a reality (Holloway, 2002, p. 223).

Miller joined the Academy because he firmly believed in higher education for black youth, and he refused to embrace Washington's model of black education as the only viable one. Booker T. Washington experienced and witnessed the terrible hardships blacks faced on a daily basis, and he understood that poverty was the main obstacle to the race's economic and civic progress. That is why Washington regarded industrial education as the best avenue for achieving both. Knowing that in the Jim Crow South and the segregated North whites opposed any kind of public education for blacks, especially liberal arts education, Washington cleverly argued that literate blacks would not become a threat to white supremacist domination, but rather, become better workers within its color-coded hierarchical structure.

Washington's educational strategy ignited a heated debate that would outlive Washington and his fiercest opponents. Most black intellectuals and scholars believed in liberal arts and industrial education, and objected to

Washington's vision in a speech many pejoratively dubbed "The Atlanta Compromise." Kelly Miller accused Washington of playing into the hands of whites, especially the philanthropists whom Washington sought to seduce in order to advance his industrial program. Miller charged that Washington's apparent willingness to sacrifice higher learning for industrial education suited the political and economic demands of his white backers and effectively barred blacks from non-industrial education altogether. Miller and other Washington critics, Alexander Crummell, W.E.B. Du Bois, and William Monroe Trotter, to name but a few, felt deeply disenchanted at what they regarded as treason to the race; for them, the "Wizard of Tuskegee" had traded the race's civil rights for economic uplift. Like many of his peers, Miller thought that the race needed more lofty aspirations than those Washington proposed.

Crummell led the charge against Washington's designs, calling industrial education for blacks that "miserable fad of industrialism" (Moss, 1981, p. 22). When Crummell passionately denounced "a set of black opportunists who will jump at anything a white man says, if it will give him notoriety and help him jingle a few nickels in his pocket," (Moss, 1981, p. 22) there was little doubt among his audience that he was speaking of the principal of Tuskegee. As president of the Academy, Crummell delivered its first address, "Civilization, The Primal Need of the Race," (Crummell, 1897) during which he outlined his philosophy of black education. Crummell averred, "Some of our leaders and teachers boldly declare, now, that *property* is the source of power; and then, the *money* is the thing which commands respect. Blind men!" (Oldfield, 1995, p. 197). To the contrary, Crummell insisted that what the race needed most was "trained and scholarly men to employ their knowledge and culture and teaching to guide both the opinions and habits of the crude masses" (Oldfield, 1995, p. 198). Alexander Crummell's unexpected death on September 10, 1898 took Kelly Miller and the other members of the Academy by surprise, but they persisted in their opposition to Washington.

A BALANCING ACT FOR THE SAKE OF RACIAL PROGRESS AND RACIAL UNITY

By the end of the Gilded Age, Kelly Miller had emerged as a worthy, cautious, and unfailingly courteous opponent of Washington's vision. Miller most notably came to the attention of Washington's camp in March 1899 when

T. Thomas Fortune, the editor of the *New York Age* and a close acquaintance of Booker T. Washington, alerted the Wizard to the young Howard academic. Fortune wrote to the Wizard that it had become necessary to "muzzle Kelly Miller" lest he "will injure Hampton and the industrial interests" (Harlan, 1975, p. 49). Agreeing with Fortune, Washington responded, "I have noted for some time with a great deal of sadness the harm which Kelly Miller [is] likely to do to the cause of industrial education" (Harlan, 1975, p. 53). Washington concluded, "I think it was a great blunder for Kelly Miller to have spoken in Boston at that Hampton meeting. His political opinions have no concern whatever with the cause of industrial education. If such influences are to control the Hampton Conference I fear that it will do me and you little good to go there" (Harlan, 1975, p. 53). Kelly Miller's friendship with Du Bois and his belief that blacks were entitled to pursue higher aspirations rather than the industrial education envisioned at Tuskegee proved to Washington's camp that Miller was a potential opponent who had to be watched closely.

While Miller may have opposed Washington's model as the only educational path, he believed that black education needed to be dual in its objectives. Refusing the either-or proposition of industrial education versus the liberal arts, Miller's answer was to privilege both. He was convinced that each served an equally important function in the advancement of the race. Born a slave, like Washington, Miller was not inclined to side with the Wizard on the basis of shared experience or misplaced sentimentalism. On the other hand, Miller also refused to exclusively support Du Bois' demands for higher learning for blacks, demands he regarded as impractical if not unattainable in the short term.

Kelly Miller (1902) first outlined his educational philosophy in detail in "The Education of the Negro," a study published in the *Report of the Commissioner of Education for the Year 1900-1901*. This report was Miller's first in-depth sociological inquiry into the race question and its publication marked a turning point in his career. Miller insisted that the primary function of education was to teach blacks the achievements of their race, "however insignificant these may appear in the eyes of his white neighbor" (Miller, 1902, p. 793). According to Miller, learning of the race's history and achievements would foster a sense of pride and promote self-worth among people who had been cast aside from the grand American narrative. For Miller, blacks had to reclaim their past in order to create a group identity that did not solely rest on the experience of enslavement, racial inferiority, and oppression. In Miller's opinion, fostering a sense of racial achievement, particularly for black children, was the first step toward education and in solving the economic, political, and social problems of the race. In addition to articulating the necessity of racial self-esteem, Miller's educational philosophy also focused on the need for both industrial and higher education because, "The higher and industrial education are not mutually exclusive, and neither can properly be played off against the other. They are both essential to the symmetrical development of any people" (Miller, 1902, p. 817). Deeply concerned that the debate about education for blacks had become increasingly personal between two equally strong-minded men, Miller remained hopeful the objective all intellectuals shared then, racial progress, could be achieved while maintaining racial cohesion.

However, Kelly Miller's efforts to reconcile both Washington's and Du Bois' philosophies proved a difficult exercise, and at times Miller's case for industrial education appears rather contradictory and elitist (Miller, 1902). Miller believed that since the overwhelming majority of blacks still lived in the rural South, industrial schools were essential for training the teachers and educators needed to enlighten the masses and expose them to Anglo-Saxon culture. In essence, industrial education was an essential part of Miller's vision about social engineering. Miller wrote, "The chief value of the mechanical and industrial schools in the South is that they inculcate in the minds of the crude agricultural population notions of thrift, economy, decency, and not because they teach the mechanical and scientific trades" (Miller, 1902, p. 820).

Miller explained how the graduates of Tuskegee, Hampton, and other industrial schools "are for the most part engaged in teaching school" (Miller, 1902, p. 820). He rightly noted,

> "I venture the assertion that not one such graduate in ten finds an opportunity to apply the trades he learned in school" (Miller, 1902, p. 820). Recent historians Henry Allen Bullock and James Anderson have agreed with Miller's observations. In their studies both Bullock (1967) and Anderson (1988) found that most of Hampton and Tuskegee graduates were more likely to become teachers than to turn to the trades or to business, a fact many of Du Bois' friends and associates refused to publicly admit (Anderson, 1988; Bullock, 1967).

While Miller acknowledged the necessity of industrial education, he did not endorse the Hampton/Tuskegee educational model in its entirety either. Instead, Miller commented on what he regarded as the weaknesses of that model. He argued that industrial education could not provide blacks avenues to success in the trades and that it was certainly not the panacea for the race's economic ills. Miller found that for graduates of industrial education schools, both business and the trades were dead ends. In theory, graduates of schools such as Hampton or Tuskegee were qualified to seek manufacturing jobs; however, Kelly Miller noted that it was nearly impossible for any to do so because of the violent opposition of white labor. Industrial education alone, like higher education, Miller asserted, could not fully respond to black economic aspirations. For Miller, industrial education was chiefly to provide the black masses with a modicum of education, which would be dispensed by the graduates of institutions like Tuskegee (Bullock, 1967, p. 188).

As for the question of higher education, Miller passionately argued, "Why should his [the African American's] education be circumscribed and limited? Why should the larger element of his nature be left unnurtured, while the mechanical side only is developed? Life is more than meat. As important as the material element is in our civilization, there is danger of pushing it too far. The highest possessions of man do not consist in material wealth" (Miller, 1902, p. 821). Agreeing with both Du Bois and William Monroe Trotter, Miller dismissed Washington's claim that black material progress was the only and safest avenue leading to political rights and to full citizenship. He wrote, "The Negro cries for justice and is offered a trade; he pleads for righteous laws, and is given an industrial school. The case is wrongly diagnosed; the remedy does not apply to the disease. It is sometimes urged upon the Negro to get money as the surest means of solving the race problem. Those who argue thus show themselves ignorant of the law of moral reforms. In all the history of the human race, the possession of money has never corrected an evil or a wrong" (Miller, 1902, p. 821). In Miller's mind, the function of higher education was clear. The college-educated black person was to officiate as a "group leader; the man who set the ideals of the community where he lives, directs its thought, and heads its social movements" (Miller, 1902, p. 840).

Unlike what earlier historians have emphasized, Kelly Miller was not a lone voice advocating the dual value and importance of both types of education. William S. Scarborough, vice president of Wilberforce University and member of the American Negro Academy, was among those whose loyalties and beliefs belonged to neither Washington's or to Du Bois' camp. Scarborough shared most of Kelly Miller's views on education. In "*The Educated Negro and His Mission*," in agreement with Miller, Scarborough (1903) noted that although the usefulness of manual training could not be questioned, there was at the same time an undeniable need for higher learning because it was the educated black woman or man's purpose to take up the leadership of its race because the time of ignorant black leadership is rapidly passing (Ronnick, 2006).

Scarborough agreed with Miller and the black elite that the main function of the college-educated African American was that of an active race leader (Gaines, 1996). Again, like Miller, Scarborough attempted to reconcile Washington and Du Bois' positions; he urged both men to respect each other's opinions and work together in order that neither [type of education] would fall to the way side (Ronnick, 2006). Scarborough added, "There is no time to lose, none to waste in eternal strife. The field is large enough for all to glean and work in. The race must make a common cause, meet a common enemy and win common friends" (Ronnick, 2006, p. 227).

For men like Miller and Scarborough who adopted a middle ground position, 1903 was a watershed year, marking the irreversible deterioration of the relationship between the Washington and Du Bois camps. Du Bois' sharp criticism of Washington's philosophy in an essay published in *The Souls of Black Folks* (Du Bois, 1903) entitled, "Of Mr. Washington and Others," sent shock waves through the Tuskegee machine and its backers, as well as through the rest of the black intelligentsia. Du Bois accused Washington and his backers of undermining blacks' efforts to secure full political rights by undercutting liberal arts education. What blacks demanded, Du Bois wrote, was the strict application of the 15th Amendment and the Civil Rights Act of 1875. Du Bois' claims were neither new nor any more radical than those made by Kelly Miller just a year earlier in his *Report of the Commissioner of Education for the Year 1900-1901* (Miller, 1902).

After 1903 Washington viewed Du Bois as an implacable foe, but the Wizard reacted to Miller differently; he found the Howard professor's approach to education more balanced and less critical of Tuskegee and of himself. While Du Bois' critique of Washington included bitter personal attacks, Miller refused to let his feelings about Washington cloud his intellectual judgment about the value of industrial education. In Miller's mind, the principal of Tuskegee was not the cause of the problems blacks faced in general and in getting access to education in particular; it was the economic, political, and racial system created and sustained by white America. Du Bois on the other hand chose to concentrate his ire on Washington, whom he regarded as the embodiment of the subservient black leader who would undermine the race in the name of getting the support of white philanthropists.

The black press soon joined the fray. Most editors favored Washington's program because it was more practical than that of Du Bois'. An editorial published in the September 1903 issue of *The Outlook* reflects that stance (anonymous, 1903, p. 74). The editorial compared *The Soul of Black Folks* (Du Bois, 1903) and Washington's *The Future of the American Negro*

(Washington, 1900) emphasizing the advantages and the practicalities of the Wizard's philosophy while ridiculing Du Bois'. Calling Du Bois a race hater, the author exhorted readers to, "Seek education—first, last, and all the time. But do not fall into the notion that education means the ability to read and understand Homer and Dante. Do not let Professor Du Bois' picture of Socrates and Francis of Assisi deceive you. The first duty of every man is to earn his living" (anonymous, 1903, p. 74). The editorial justified its position by asking with biting irony, "Is this materialism? Very well! Materialism is the basis of life" (anonymous, 1903, p. 74). All the while Miller, horrified by such a display of division, remained silent on the onslaught against Du Bois. Miller refused to engage in public warfare with either camp, mainly because he prized racial unity above public disagreements. It is in that spirit that he continued to reach out to both groups.

THE PERILS OF KELLY MILLER'S INCLUSIVE EDUCATIONAL VISION

In the early months of 1903, Washington planned a conference on education policy to be held in New York City in 1904, financed by steel tycoon Andrew Carnegie. In preparation for that conference, Du Bois drew up an educational platform that mirrored Kelly Miller's. In a confidential letter to Miller, Du Bois highlighted his ten-point platform that emphasized higher learning for a selected few, industrial and universal education for the masses. Since Du Bois' program was very similar to his own, Miller lent his support to Du Bois' agenda. Washington got wind of this alliance and decided not to invite Miller to the conference, despite Du Bois' determination that Miller must attend. The Harvard graduate began to lobby on Miller's behalf and Washington's camp escalated. In April, Miller lamented, "Is it war to the knife, and knife to the hilt?" (Lewis, 1993, p. 309). After nearly a year of frustrating, painstakingly arduous, and often acrimonious negotiations, the meeting was finalized. Washington relented and Miller was invited to the conference. Ironically, after seven months of intense negotiation to include Miller, Du Bois began to have misgivings about the meeting. An optimistic Miller tried to convince Du Bois that "Our local conference I fear is almost a matter of 'help me Cassius or I sink'. I am glad that Mr. W will be present. I do not think that the conference will be stampeded by his presence" (Harlan and Smock, 1977b, p. 330). Miller thought that the meeting would soothe the relations between the two men and provide an avenue to discuss their views and methods about how best to achieve full citizenship for all blacks.

The conference was held in New York from January 6-8, 1904. According to biographer David Lewis (1993), Du Bois' fear of being isolated and manipulated by members of the Washington camp was soon confirmed (Lewis, 1993, p. 306). Washington's mastery at putting forth a seemingly conciliatory agenda had appealed to Miller, who longed to find common ground and bury the hatchet (Harlan and Smock, 1977a). Believing that Washington was sincere and wanting to end the strife tearing the black intelligentsia apart, Miller and his associate, Archibald Grimke, convinced themselves that ending the internecine warfare was worth a few concessions from both sides. For taking this stance they have been branded by Lewis (1993) as, "The Miller camp of straddlers" (Lewis, 1994, p. 306).

The New York meeting ended with the creation of a Committee of Twelve that was to be presided under the joint leadership of Washington and Du Bois. Kelly Miller, Archibald Grimke, and T. Thomas Fortune were also appointed to the committee. Even though Miller was on the committee, Du Bois felt isolated and became convinced that Washington plotted his sequestration in order to circumvent him. He later told Miller and Grimke that Washington planned to "have me at his mercy by simply having his men out vote me" (Aptheker, 1973, p. 105). Despite the fact that Grimke and Miller remained on good terms with Washington, Du Bois did not regard the pair as straddlers; in fact, the relationship between Miller and Du Bois was initially unscathed by the fractious politicking surrounding the formation of the Committee of Twelve.

After Du Bois published "The Parting of the Ways," in the April 1904 issue of *World Today*, the divorce from Booker T. Washington became final (Aptheker, 1973, p. 81). Du Bois canceled a trip to New York, where he was to attend the July meeting of the Committee. His absence was interpreted as a *de facto* resignation and allowed Washington to establish himself as the chairman. Du Bois' worst fears materialized when Kelly Miller not only stayed on the committee, but he agreed to become secretary of the committee, and Archibald Grimke became its treasurer. A month later, refusing to make amends despite Miller's pleas, Du Bois officially resigned from the Committee.

Overtime, it became clear to Miller that Booker T. Washington had no intention of instituting reforms in his leadership style or of addressing the criticisms lodged against his educational model, yet Miller remained on the Committee, as did Grimke. Miller still believed that he could be an honest broker between the two factions and perhaps positively influence Washington. In an earlier effort to deter Du Bois from resigning, Miller and Grimke had emphasized practicality instead of passion and an attachment to inflexible principles. The two men argued that although the Committee of Twelve did not meet their expectations either, it was "the only efficient active force in the field" (Aptheker, 1973, p. 112). Both thought that in spite of its shortcomings, the committee could provide a venue for the two camps to work out an agenda for black education and other economic, social, and political issues. Miller was also keen to preserve intra-racial unity. Miller's and Grimke's arguments did not sway Du Bois in the least. He explained his decision, writing to Miller and Grimke, "There was one course left to me and that was to resign. That I did. Under no circumstances will I withdraw it. I refuse to wear Mr. Washington's livery, or put on his collar" (Aptheker, 1973, p. 105). Historians regard Du Bois' resignation as a testament to his determination to stay true to his principles. On the other hand, Miller's decision not to resign led his contemporaries and historians to brand him as a "straddler," one who was disloyal, weak, or opportunistic.

The New York meeting solidified Washington's position as the president of black affairs and cemented the rift between Washington and Du Bois. The Committee of Twelve incident also damaged the relationship between Miller, Grimke, and Du Bois. While Du Bois felt betrayed by Miller and Grimke, the pair was puzzled and angered by Du Bois' resignation, which was a surprise to them both. Miller and Grimke thought that Du Bois had acted prematurely and that his resignation served no positive purpose: "We are frank to say that your sudden and unexplained withdrawal from a compact of your own devising would seem to lay you liable to the charge of bad faith; and, as you know, your opponents are ready to exploit the charge" (Fox, 1971, p. 87). Miller was perhaps most displeased by Du Bois' decision to leave the committee because it was only after strong and persistent pressure from Du Bois that Miller had relented and agreed to participate in the conference in the first place. In spite of their differences—in typical conciliatory Miller fashion—Miller continued to cooperate with Du Bois to insure that higher education would be an option for black youth, which meant that he would have to go against Booker T. Washington periodically.

MANAGING DISSENT

In January 1905, Miller and Bishop Alexander Walters organized a group of anti-Tuskegee leaders who planned to meet with President Theodore Roosevelt to demonstrate to him that there was diversity of opinion in matters of racial uplift and that Booker T. Washington was not the sole voice of black America. Washington's allies closely monitored Kelly Miller and his fellow conspirators and the Wizard learned that a memorandum was sent to the president outlining the group's demands. Uncharacteristically, for those who see him as a straddler, Miller played a central role in the whole affair, as most meetings were held at his house near the Howard University campus. One of Washington's acquaintances communicated to him the partial list of the members of the group. Washington regarded those who had been excluded as belonging to the Tuskegee camp.

Notwithstanding situational cooperation like that demonstrated in the Roosevelt meeting, the tension between Miller, Grimke, and Du Bois created by Du Bois' resignation did not subside. Du Bois' bruised ego is evidenced by his decision to exclude both Miller and Grimke from the first meeting of the Niagara Movement, scheduled for July 1905 in Buffalo, New York. Du Bois later explained his decision: "You both belong to Mr. Washington's committee and membership in both organizations seemed to me inconsistent" (Aptheker, 1973, p 113). Du Bois' decision, dictated by his anger and his resentment toward two close associates whom he thought had betrayed him, was a slap in the face intended to inflict equal embarrassment on Miller and Grimke. Miller felt deeply wronged by Du Bois, and when Du Bois hastily invited both he and Grimke to attend the second meeting of the movement late that summer, it was by then much too late to mend fences. Du Bois tried to sway Miller by emphasizing the quality and integrity of the group, writing, "I was not sure that I would find 50 men who had not bowed the knee to Baal. Today we have a growing enthusiastic organization of nearly 75 members, educated, determined and unpurchasable men" (Aptheker, 1973, p. 113). For once, Miller was devoid of his customary spirit of conciliation. Refusing to forgive what he considered a grave insult, Miller took a firm stand that many of his critics should have applauded. He did not go to Harper's Ferry and Grimke followed suit.

The Niagara Movement's Declaration of Principles, issued in the summer of 1905, included a section on education, which demanded that common schooling be free and compulsory for all American children and emphasized that college training should not be the sole right of any single group or class in a country (Marrable, 2009). The declaration stressed the need to increase public funding for education, particularly in the South. In the September 1905 issue of *The Voice of the Negro,* Du Bois asserted that the right to vote and the opposition to any form of discrimination, including in the legal process, were the cornerstones of the Niagara Movement's charter.

The platform promulgated by the movement probably held some appeal for Kelly Miller, especially its position on education, but joining Du Bois' organization from the start would have meant forgiving the humiliation inflicted by one whom he had considered a friend and an ally. Moreover, if he had joined the group then Washington would have interpreted it as an unequivocal alliance with the Monroe Trotter and Du Bois forces. It was not the fear of retaliation from Washington that stopped Miller but rather, Du Bois' association with William Monroe Trotter, the very prickly, firebrand editor of *The Boston Guardian.* Because of his personality and his antagonistic editorials, Trotter was not the kind of man with whom Miller wanted to keep close company. Miller was not alone in his characterizing of Trotter as a loose cannon; the consensus among black intellectuals and leaders was that Trotter was simply too rash and unpredictable. Philanthropist and activist Oswald Garrison Villard, a believer of racial progress and a supporter of Booker T. Washington, considered Trotter to be dangerous (Aptheker, 1973).

Miller especially objected to Trotter's personalization of the education and racial uplift debates, allowing his enmity for Washington to supersede the agenda of the movement. "His every utterance leads to the Cato-like refrain 'Booker Washington must be destroyed,'" Miller lamented (Miller, 1908, p. 14). Miller's criticism went even further when he claimed that many of the subscribers to the Niagara movement had not, up to that time, been known for their activism on behalf of the race, and that the group was "a cult" with all the zeal and intolerance typical of new converts (Miller, 1908, p. 16).

Miller's initial unequivocal disapproval of the Niagara Movement is also apparent when he noted that "The platform of the movement contained nothing new, and its dynamic was derived from dissent" (Miller, 1908, p. 16). Even after Du Bois' attempts at reconciliation, Miller remained convinced that the Niagara Movement did not add anything to the goals of the Committee of Twelve, but instead undermined its credibility and its potential for success by fracturing the black intelligentsia instead of fostering race unity. Furthermore, Kelly Miller still believed that much of the tension between Washington and Du Bois was more a mere "difference of point of view" (Miller, 1908, p. 24), rather than "an irrepressible conflict" (Miller, 1908, p. 24). In fact, Miller thought, "The subject of industrial and higher education is merely one of ratio and proportion, and not one of fundamental controversy" (Miller, 1908, p. 19).

Even though Miller's criticism of Du Bois and Trotter was harsh, he was no gentler with Booker T. Washington. In "Radicals and Conservatives," Miller wrote that while Washington was indeed a "diplomat, and a great one," (Miller, 1908, p. 20) he was "a practical opportunist, accepting the best terms…" (Miller, 1908, p. 18). Miller also chastised the Wizard for being a pawn of southern whites in their determination to deny black claims to higher education and to full citizenship. Miller concluded bitterly that "The whites have set up Booker Washington as in a former day they set up Frederick Douglass, as the divinely appointed and anointed leader of his race, and regard as sacrilege all criticism and even candid discussion on the part of those whom he has been sent to guide" (Miller, 1908, p. 21). Once more, secure in his belief that both higher and industrial education were equally beneficial to blacks, and that the race needed its leaders for all their failings, to unite rather than lose track of the greater good of the race because of endless bickering, Miller refused to side with either camp. He would go on, for the remainder of his life, arguing that both kinds of education were essential for black individual and collective success.

Like both Washington and Du Bois, Miller continued to regard education as the most essential part of the agenda to obtain full citizenship and economic progress. He argued, "Education must accomplish more for a backward people than it does for those who are in the fore front of progress" (Miller, 1905, p. 13). Like his intellectual counterparts, Miller believed that education was "the only gateway by which a new people may enter civilization" (Miller, 1905, p. 15). He was convinced that there was an equal need for both vocational and liberal arts education because each addressed a different but equally fundamental need of the race. Miller could not imagine Du Bois' crusade for full citizenship being a successful one in the foreseeable future, and he thought that until such an end could be achieved, the alternative Washington's program offered was not to be disregarded on principle alone. Miller constantly urged black leaders to acknowledge the economic hurdles African Americans faced and the realities of the labor market. In Miller's opinion, for most blacks, practical training was a necessity rather than a choice. Miller deplored the fact that Du Bois and his associates seemed oblivious to the economic conditions black men, women, and children faced daily. He wrote, "Advocacy of adequate preparation for immediate and available service on the part of those who can secure no other is in no sense inconsistent with the higher needs and aspirations of the race" (Miller, 1908, pp. 177).

To the end, Miller believed that both forms of education were valuable for blacks because they were interconnected, the former providing the latter with the indispensable leadership needed for the race's uplift. Was not Booker T. Washington himself an educated Negro, Miller asked? And was he not "The great apostle of industrial training" (Miller, 1905, p. 32)? Miller asserted that since Jim Crow was a fact that could be neither ignored nor changed at the present time, and because most Southern states had legislated against white professors and teachers working in black institutions, there was an undeniable need to train black teachers. These teachers, Miller argued, should be trained at vocational schools like Tuskegee, as was already the case.

While clearly seeing the virtues of Washington's industrial education, Miller shared Du Bois' conviction that an educated elite was imperative if blacks were to achieve equality, and that this elite would come from black schools. "The social separation of the races in America renders it imperative that the professional classes among the Negroes should be recruited from their own ranks" (Miller, 1908, p. 26). Black teachers educated in the cities would go to the most remote rural areas of the South to educate the masses (Miller, 1903, p. 128). Kelly Miller insisted that "A more enlightened leadership" should guide the masses toward accepting the realities of the race situation and encouraged them to be practical until Jim Crow could effectively be defeated (Miller, 1903, p. 177).

THE CONTROVERSY ENDS

The personal warfare between Washington and Du Bois ended with the Wizard's death in 1915. When Washington passed away, so did much of the spirit of accommodation he championed. While the hot fire of the great educational debate cooled with the death of one of its chief antagonists, the debate did go on—and in the direction predicted and favored by Kelly Miller. Southern school districts began to raise their standards for teacher certification, for both black and white instructors. Unfortunately, for those white southerners who would confine blacks to industrial education, schools of the Hampton and Tuskegee variety did a poor job of preparing black students to meet the new standards. Whites had one of two choices: they could either raise the academic standards of the industrial arts schools, or have white instructors teach in the region's black primary and secondary schools. While the latter course would have allowed whites to maintain control of the black student population, it would have undermined the Jim Crow system that was firmly in place in the early 20th century. To preserve that system, white legislators and philanthropists began to encourage more liberal arts education at industrial arts schools.

At the same time, the death of "The Great Accommodator" ushered in the era of the "New Negro," with Du Bois as its chief propagandist. Black college students were no longer content with the dead-end careers a Tuskegee education prepared them for, so they began to agitate for still higher academic standards. Students at both Fisk and Hampton were successful in having their paternalistic white presidents removed from office during the 1920s. If the "New Negroes" had their way, industrial education would have passed away with Booker T. Washington and Miller's pragmatism would have been viewed as the wrong strategy for the times; unfortunately, it was not up to them.

White industrial philanthropists and the General Education Board funded black education in the South. These white men acknowledged that the liberal arts would have to be taught to a degree—even at industrial education institutions—to ensure that there would be enough black teachers for black schools. Furthermore, they still believed that practical education was best for the black masses, and that if done properly, a smattering of liberal arts education would produce a black leadership class that would inculcate in their constituencies the ways of accommodation and moderation. So these men insisted upon combining elements of liberal arts and industrial arts at those schools they funded, most of the private schools in the South, schools that were the basis of black education. Educators like Kelly Miller, William Scarborough of Morehouse College and Atlanta University President John Hope, were left no choice but to steer a middle course to keep the doors of their schools open to prepare those students who would be leaders during the Civil Rights era (Anderson, 1988). This compromise was not one that black intellectual and educational leaders would have chosen, but is the one that allowed the race to move forward. In the end, that was Kelly Miller's point: in a perfect world blacks could pursue their ideals and live according to their truest principles, but that world did not yet exist in Jim Crow America. Until racial justice and equality became national realities—indeed to make their arrival possible—blacks would have to seize all opportunities for advancement that were available to them. Miller knew that there was no one correct way of achieving equality, and that blacks had to move ahead on all fronts, moving fastest where there was least opposition and slower in those areas where there was more resistance—and then shifting gears when necessary and going in the other direction. For Kelly Miller, refusing to be boxed in by ideology was not "straddling"; it was common sense. Future generations could have learned a great deal from Miller, given the battles that lay ahead over integration and Black Nationalism, the Republican Party versus the Democratic Party, and black liberals versus black conservatives. Unfortunately, because he cared more for results than posturing, he has been relegated to the margins of black history. Perhaps a new generation is ready to learn from this great black intellectual.

REFERENCES

Anonymous. (1903). Two typical leaders. *The Outlook, 74*(4), 214-216.

Anderson, J. D. (1988). *The education of blacks in the south, 1860-1935*. Chapel Hill: University of North Carolina Press.

Aptheker, H. (Ed.). (1968). *A documentary history of the Negro people in the United States*. New York: Citadel Press.

Aptheker, H. (Ed.). (1973). *The correspondence of W. E. B. Du Bois: Selections, 1877-1934*. Amherst: The University of Massachusetts Press.

Banks, W. M. (1998). *Black intellectuals: Race and responsibility in American life*. New York. W.W. Norton and Co.

Bullock, H. A. (1967). *A history of Negro education in the south: From 1619 to the present*. Cambridge: Harvard University Press.

Crummell, A. (1897). Civilization the primal need of the race. *The American Negro Academy, Occasional Papers, 3*, 3-7.

Du Bois, W.E.B. (1903). *The souls of black folk*. Chicago: A.C. McClurg.

Du Bois, W.E.B. (1904, April). The parting of ways. *World Today*, 521-532.

Du Bois, W.E.B, (1905, September). The Niagara movement. *The Voice of the Negro,*622-629.

Eisenberg, B. (1960). Kelly Miller: The Negro leader as a marginal man. *The Journal of Negro History, 45*(3),182-197.

Fox, S. R. (1971). *The guardian of Boston: William Monroe Trotter*. New York: Athenum.

Gatewood, W. B. (1990). *Aristocrats of color, the black elite, 1880-1920*. Bloomington: Indiana University Press.

Harlan, L. R. (1975). *Booker T. Washington: Volume 1: The making of a black leader, 1856-1901*. New York: Oxford University Press.

Harlan, L.R., and Smock, R.W. (Eds.). (1975). *The Booker T. Washington papers, volume 4: 1859-1898*. Urbana-Champaign: The University of Illinois Press.

Harlan, L. R., and Smock, R. W. (Eds.). (1977a). *The Booker T Washington papers, volume 5: 1899-1900.* Urbana-Champaign: The University of Illinois Press.

Harlan, L. R., and Smock, R. W. (Eds.). (1977b). *The Booker T. Washington papers, volume 7: 1903-1904.* Urbana Champaign: The University of Illinois Press.

Harlan, L. R. (1986). *Booker T. Washington: Volume 2: The wizard of Tuskegee.* New York: Oxford University Press.

Holloway, J. S. (2002). *Confronting the veil, Abram Harris Jr., E. Franklin Frazier and Ralph Bunche, 1919-1941.* Chapel Hill: University of North Carolina Press.

Lewis, D. L. (1993). *W.E.B. Du Bois, 1868-1919: Biography of a race.* New York: Henry Holt.

Marable, M. (2009). *Let nobody turn us around: Voices of resistance, reform, and renewal.* Lanham: Rowman and Littelfield.

Meier, A. (1960). The racial and educational philosophy of Kelly Miller. *The Journal of Negro Education, 29*(2), 21-127.

Meier, A. (1966). *Negro thought in America, 1880-1915.* Ann Arbor: Michigan University Press.

Miller, K. (1902). *The education of the Negro. Report of the commissioner of education for the Year 1900-190 (Volume 1).* Washington: Government Printing Office.

Miller, K. (1905). *Howard University: From servitude to service (Being the old south lectures on the history and work of southern institutions for the education of the Negro).* Boston: American Unitarian Association.

Miller, K. (1908). *Race adjustment, essays on the Negro in America.* New York and Washington: H.E. Neal Publishing Co.

Moss. A. A. Jr. (1981). *American Negro academy: Voice of the talented tenth.* Baton Rouge: Louisiana University Press.

Olfield, J. R. (Ed.). (1995*). Civilization and black progress: Selected writings of Alexander Crummell on the south.* Charlottesville: University of Virginia Press.

Ronnick, M. V. (Ed.). (2006). *The selected writings of William Sanders Scarborough.* New York: Oxford University Press.

Scarborough, W. (1903). The educated Negro and his mission. *American Negro Academy, Occasional Papers,* 8, 3-11.

Washington, B.T. (1902). *The future of the American Negro*. Boston: Small, Maynard and Company.

Washington, B. T. (1919). *Up from slavery: An autobiography*. New York: Doubleday and Pace Company.

Chapter 3

EDUCATION AND THE INTELLIGENCE ASSESSMENT OF AFRICAN AMERICANS, 1917–1945

Cameron Seay

INTRODUCTION

Historically, the world economy has demanded systems of education and innovation to produce complex civilizations. In schools, educators were able to recognize and validate the intellectual abilities of students to offer them appropriate instruction or training. To build these educational systems, it was unavoidable that we made certain assumptions about the nature of teaching, learning, thinking, and knowing (Greeno, et al., 1996).

In the U.S., our assumptions about the nature of intelligence – how to identify and measure it – have come from a national psychology of racial and ethnic relations, which has evolved over time in a social context. These assumptions about the capacities of minority students are today the driving force behind teacher practices, students' learning, and student assessment. The general beliefs about students' performance have congealed into the current thinking (wholly unsubstantiated) that we can administer a single test to make a global determination about one's level of intelligence or school achievement. Our tool for this task has become high-stakes standardized tests. A single number on a single test determines many students' prospects in life, and the educational orthodoxy generally accepts this as valid. But is it?

In this chapter, I provide a historical context for some of the assumptions and beliefs that drive today's education. I explain the evolution of education and mental testing in regards to the racialization of the nation. This chapter seeks to build awareness regarding the substantial body of literature on intelligence testing, which advanced the belief in the intellectual superiority of whites over blacks.

I offer a brief review of the period prior to 1917, and the events that led up to the mass intelligence testing that began in that year. I then review, in some detail, the most relevant literature of the period 1917-1945, regarding intelligence testing as it is related to African Americans. I focus on the move towards mass intelligence testing in America and the presumption of intellectual superiority, on which testing was premised. I investigate the rich body of literature generated between the 1920s and 1940s that provided a powerful refutation of the superiority presumption. This body of literature is not widely known among academics (most psychologists and educators do not know of it), but in terms of design and scholarly discourse, it is among the finest literature ever generated by the social sciences in this country. Using the *Journal of Negro Education* as a forum, this group of scholars did more than bring into serious question the work of Henry Goddard, Lewis Terman, Robert Yerkes, and those who followed them— work that was, and is still taken as having complete validity among mainstream social scientists. These scholars brought into question the very foundations of American psychology and education: that "intelligence" can be measured by a single, linear value and that whites were innately intellectually superior to blacks or "Negroes," as the literature of the time identified the people we now call African Americans.

ORIGINS OF INTELLIGENCE TESTING IN AMERICA

The intellectual pioneer of intelligence testing was most likely Francis Galton (1822-1911). In his books *Hereditary Genius* (Galton, 1869) and *Inquiries Into Human Faculty and its Development* (1883), Galton explained his view that intellectual ability was limited to a few illustrious white families (one of which, of course, was his own). He was convinced that intelligence was almost completely hereditary in nature, and that there was little one could do to improve intellectual ability via education (Galton, 1869).

In stark contrast to the work of Galton was that of Alfred Binet (1857-1911), who was convinced that intellectual ability was a function of circumstance - including, and perhaps most importantly, education. His best-known work, *The Development of Intelligence in Children* (Binet, 1916/1973), clearly outlines his philosophy that it is environment that primarily drives an individual's intellectual profile, and that this profile can be dramatically modified through education.

The legacy of Francis Galton (and very indirectly that of Binet) led to the emergence of a body of literature among psychologists that supported and reflected American mores and perceptions about "race." The earliest "intelligence test" that addressed the issue of race we know of is that given in 1897 by G. R. Stetson (Wiggan, 2007). Stetson tested 500 African Americans and 500 white children in the public schools of Washington, D. C. (Guthrie, 1998). The test used poetry: the experimenter read a poem out loud and the subjects tried to repeat what was read. In this particular test, the African American children outperformed their white peers (p. 63). Strong (1913) and Pyle (1915) also gave intelligence tests based on race, and in both cases, the white participants outperformed their black peers.

However, it was the work of three men, Henry Goddard (1856-1957), Lewis Terman (1877-1956), and Robert Yerkes (1876-1956), which laid the foundation for the mass intelligence testing that began in the 1920s. Goddard worked at the Training School for Feeble-minded Girls and Boys at Vineland, New Jersey. Terman worked at Stanford and Yerkes worked at Harvard. All three were convinced that intelligence was, more or less, fixed at birth. All three were clear in their belief that whites were inherently the intellectual superiors to blacks (Goddard, 1920; Terman, 1916/1975; Yerkes, 1921).

Like many who believed that intelligence was fixed at birth, all three men were greatly influenced by Galton and indirectly influenced by Binet. Goddard actually provided the first known translation of Binet's work into English from the original French (Fancher, 1985). Terman created an individually administered intelligence test that he claimed was based on Binet's work. It was not. Goddard and Terman's view of intelligence as being rigidly quantifiable and fixed was antithetical to that of Binet. Yerkes took the method of testing developed by Terman and modified it for mass administration. This test became the Army Mental Tests, Alpha and Beta. The Army Mental Tests were administered to over 1.5 million men beginning in 1917, and was an early precursor for our standardized testing method today. One of Yerkes' assistants, Carl Brigham, was instrumental in the development of the Scholastic Aptitude Test (SAT). Of course, the Army Mental Tests established, beyond the shadow of any doubt as far as the American public was concerned, that whites were the clear intellectual superiors of blacks. That the tests were replete with methodological and common sense flaws (like the average mental age of the American male being several years below that which Terman had "scientifically" calculated years earlier) was of little importance to an America eager for a way to measure intelligence quickly. The result was a torrent of literature that supported Yerkes' findings. The only problem was that everyone, including Yerkes himself, overlooked the same error in logic: American race relations had very little, if anything, to do with genetics.

The approach taken by Strong (1913) was typical. Strong separated the "Negroes" (the term used in the research of the time) based on the lightness of their skin, applying the prevailing hypothesis that the lighter-complexioned blacks had more "white blood" in them, and, therefore, they had to be smarter than other blacks. This was an assumption that was often repeated in the research on racially based mental comparisons, which would come to be known as the "Mulatto Hypothesis" (Guthrie, 1998). It is easy for us today to see the fallacy in such thinking, but it permeated the research of the "hereditarians" (the term applied to those who felt intelligence was derived via heredity). What Strong (1913) ended up with, but did not report, were variances in performance that were actually based on differences in education and social status, not genetics. The "social factors" researchers (those who felt environment heavily influenced intellectual ability), who are discussed later, used such "intra-group" analyses to thoroughly dismantle the theories of heredity-based intelligence. Strong and many other researchers used skin complexion to determine how much "white blood" a black person possessed. They believed that the lighter complexioned African Americans were more intelligent than other blacks ("Mulatto Hypothesis"). From a scientific standpoint, these researchers could not have taken a more flawed methodological approach.

In addition to the work of Pyle (1915) and Strong (1913), other authors promoting the hereditarian view included Dagny Sunne (Sunne, 1917), Ada Hart Arlitt (Arlitt, 1921, 1922), G. O. Ferguson (Ferguson, 1921), Edward L. Thorndike (Thorndike, 1923), Guy Whipple (1923), Frederick Lamson Whitney, Florence Goodenough (Goodenough, 1926), and Paul Young (Young, 1929). Consistently, these authors' studies indicated that African Americans in most cases, scored lower on intelligence tests than whites, and that southern and darker-skinned blacks consistently scored lower than their northern and lighter-skinned counterparts. An annoying occurrence, however, was the consistency with which northern blacks scored higher than southern whites. Two interesting concepts were used to explain this anomaly: the "Mulatto Hypothesis," and the "Selective Migration" theory. As stated above, the "Mulatto Hypothesis" held that lighter skinned blacks often scored higher on intelligence tests than darker skinned blacks (especially in the South), not because of the social hierarchy, which gave them favorable treatment, but because they had more "white blood" (Peterson, 1923). On the other hand, the selective migration theory was simple (if not verifiable): the more intelligent African Americans chose to migrate to the North. Otto Klineberg would have much to say about this flawed reasoning in the 1920s and 30s.

A RESPONSE TO THE HEREDITARIANS

After the widespread use of the Army Mental Tests during WW I, the 1920s saw an explosion in the application of intelligence testing, both individually and in groups. Many new tests were created (see Shuey, 1958), and a level of acceptance arose for mass testing methods such that few questions were raised regarding the validity of the tests (Guthrie, 1998). Because such testing provided quantitative data, its scientific validity was initially, for the most part, accepted as a given by the academic community.

However, the tests, almost without exception, had a common characteristic: they were normed for whites (Guthrie, 1998). African Americans, having a very different social situation as a group, would consistently score lower than whites. This was as Binet said it would be: like a peasant, normal in ordinary surroundings of the fields, who may be considered a moron in the city (Binet & Simon, 1916/1973). Given the stature of the researchers that developed the intelligence tests, in particular Terman and Yerkes, it is little wonder that American education began to accept the tests *en masse* and *prima facie*. That the tests indicated that African American children were inherently inferior to white children, may not have added to the popularity of the tests, but it did not detract from that popularity either.

There were few black psychologists in the 1920s. Howard University had only 20 black graduate students in psychology between 1919 and 1938 (Guthrie, 1998). No other black colleges were listed as having graduate programs in psychology. In schools outside of the South (that is, schools that allowed both white and black students to matriculate together), there were listed only 31 African American graduate students, in total, between the years 1930 and 1936 (Guthrie, 1998, pp. 156-157). The first African American to be awarded a Ph.D. in psychology, Francis Sumner (a student of G. Stanly Hall at Clark University, as was Lewis Terman), did not receive his degree until 1920. Consequently, there was little argument among black scholars regarding the hereditarians' perspective of intelligence. To be sure, it would have been entirely possible for white or non-black psychologists to attack the flaws in the hereditarian position, and in fact, some did. However, until the ascendance of a new cadre of black psychologists emerged, the hereditarian position remained relatively unchallenged in the scholarly community.

In the 1920s, however, there began to emerge a voice to answer the hereditarians. Walter Lippman, the brilliant, Harvard-educated writer and social critic, wrote a series of six articles in the New Republic in the fall of 1922 (Lippman, 1922). In these articles, Lippman presented a well-crafted but scathing critique of intelligence tests—specifically the contention advanced by the Army Mental Tests that the mental age of the average adult American male was thirteen. Lippman argued: "The average adult intelligence cannot be less than the average adult intelligence..." This remark was in direct response to Yerkes's finding that the "mental age" of the average American was three years less than what Terman proposed it to be (Lippman, 1922a, p. 213).

Lippman went on through the six articles to piercingly analyze the tests of Terman and Yerkes, and pointed out their divergence from the intentions of Binet. Lippman compared the intelligence tests to measuring athletic ability, while failing to differentiate between the athletic ability of a sprinter and a weightlifter (Lippman, 1922b). Lippman's point was obvious. Because of the testers' failure to precisely define what it is that was being measured, there was no way of determining the accuracy of the measurement.

Otto Klineberg, the prolific scholar from Columbia University, wrote *An Experimental Study of Speed and Other Factors in "Racial" Differences* in 1928 (Klineberg, 1928). This was a serious attempt to challenge many of the assumptions made by the hereditarians, including the concept of "race" itself. Klineberg's contention was that social factors heavily influenced performance on intelligence tests, including: language, schooling, culture, social and economic status, rapport, and motivation (p. 6-24). He also applied, and disregarded as unsupported, the "Mulatto Hypothesis."

Klineberg used the Pintner-Paterson series (see Shuey, 1958) with Yakima Indians, blacks (in New York and rural West Virginia), and whites. He measured the speed and accuracy with which the subjects completed the tests. His conclusions were as follows: the superiority of whites over "Negroes" and Indians was in time and not performance, and this superiority was probably due to environment; other groups exhibited an equal ability to learn as whites; there was no evidence that performance increased in other groups as "white blood" increased (Klineberg, 1928, p. 107).

In addition, Kleinberg noted that the performance of the New York African Americans was higher than those in West Virginia. This he attributed not to the New York blacks having more "white blood," but to their having, in all probability, a superior educational environment. This is one of the first cases where a well-respected researcher from a leading university undertook a major study of racial differences in intelligence and concluded that these perceived differences were attributable, predominately, to environment rather than ancestry. Dagny Sunne (1917), and to a lesser extent Ada Arlitt (1922), hinted at the same conclusions Klineberg overtly stated. He would do so quite often during his long career. *An Experimental Study* represented a point of departure in the literature. The work of Arlitt and Sunne sought to respectfully investigate a premise they thought was valid (that is, race is a factor in intelligence). However, Klineberg adopted no such premise. Concepts like the "Mulatto Hypothesis" and the innate white intellectual superiority claim were critiqued methodologically. Klineberg, in some ways, created a new posture from which to address the contentions of the hereditarians – their position would be required to give an account for itself. Until the appearance of Klineberg, Lippman, and other critics in the 1920s, the hereditarians' position rested safely on the eminence of their proponents.

In 1930, Paul Witty and Harvey C. Lehman wrote an article entitled "Racial Differences: The Dogma of Racial Superiority" (Witty & Lehman, 1930). Witty was a prominent scholar from Northwestern University who would later serve as a mentor to Martin Jenkins. Lehman went on to do seminal work at Ohio University. In this article, Witty and Lehman pointed to the apparently intractable problem of differentiating environmental factors from hereditary ones. They cited numerous studies that indicated that familiarity with English was a clearly identifiable factor in how well one did on intelligence tests. They further cited numerous other studies that showed the impact of social status and education on performance on intelligence tests. Witty and Lehman also highlighted the studies and themes that supported the social factors literature. One of the major themes was that the "within-race" differences were always greater than the "between-race" differences on intelligence tests. Witty's brilliant student, Martin Jenkins, would repeatedly illustrate this in numerous intra-race studies. The importance of Witty's contribution to the social factors literature is that he was a scholar of impeccable reputation from a school of equally lofty stature. His opinion mattered, and his work was taken seriously.

African American Scholars Emerge

Though there were few black psychologists to refute the claim of the inherent intellectual inferiority of African Americans, black writers from other disciplines participated in the debate. One of these writers was Horace Mann Bond (1904-1972). Bond was a graduate of Lincoln University and the University of Chicago, where his doctorate was in education rather than psychology. Throughout his long and storied career, Bond was a consistent advocate for the education of African Americans and a prolific writer on the topic.

In 1924, while only 20 years old, Bond wrote "Intelligence Tests and Propaganda" (Bond, 1924) in which he challenged the efficacy and biased nature of the tests. In 1927, Bond wrote another article in *The Crisis*. This time, he directly addressed the contention of the hereditarians' racist claim that IQ scores proved that African Americans were innately intellectually inferior to whites. In prose that dripped with sarcasm, Bond referred to IQ testing as a type of major indoor sport among psychologists (Bond, 1927). He asked why white researchers seemed to feel that it was important for there to be rapport between white testers and white children, but they did not seem to think it was necessary to emphasize the same approach with black children. He also made mention of the fact that normed samples were always comprised of white subjects, and often exclusively from the middle and upper classes.

Bond decided to modify the research protocol that was followed almost without exception in previous intelligence testing. He set about to create a positive and comfortable environment for the students taking the test. Binet said repeatedly that this was essential (Binet, 1916/1973). They also wanted to include students from a variety of economic backgrounds, and they selected thirty schoolchildren from Chicago to meet this objective. A quiet, supportive environment was created. The environment was as close to ideal as the testers could make it.

The results were startling, at least in contrast to previous intelligence assessments of African Americans up until that time. Bond found that 63% of the black children scored above 106; in Terman's sample of white youth, 33% did so. According to Bond, only 5% of white children may be expected to equal or exceed an IQ of 122. In his test, no less than 47% of the subjects exceeded that score. While clearly not advocating for the intellectual superiority of blacks over whites, Bond did seek to point out that social circumstance, in particular access to intellectual stimulation at an early age, would boost the scores of all children (Bond, 1927, p. 259).

During this time, several black scholars were completing their training (some of them were completing their initial graduate level work) in the latter part of the 1920s, and they were preparing themselves for the contributions they would make in the decades to come. Charles Henry Thompson (1896-1980), who would later be a founding editor of the *Journal of Negro Education* at Howard University, graduated from the University of Chicago in 1925 with a doctorate in educational psychology. Thompson would be an important figure in the body of research that countered the hereditarians' arguments.

In 1928 Thompson published, "The Educational Achievements of Negro Children" (Thompson, 1928). He deployed what was for the time a novel tactic. Instead of operating under the assumption that white children were inherently superior to black children, Thompson made a concerted effort to assume that children from both races came into the world with more or less the same intellectual ability. Thompson proposed that:

> It is the purpose of this paper, in the second place, therefore, to point out the *conditioning* effect of the assumption of an inherent inferiority of the Negro by predicating our analysis upon the opposite premise; namely, that the Negro child is equal to the white child in mental and scholastic abilities, and that such differences as arise are due to environment. (Thompson, 1928, p. 194)

"The Educational Achievements of Negro Children" was an extensive critique of the methods that were being used to assess black intelligence. It was clear to Thompson that any evaluation of African Americans' academic achievement was "inextricably" intertwined with racial stratification in America (Thompson, 1928, p. 193). It was also clear to him that the socio-economic statuses resulting from this racial stratification were primary driving forces behind the perceived intellectual differences between blacks and whites. He concludes:

1. That the doctrine of an inherent mental inferiority of the "Negro" is a myth unfounded by the most logical interpretation of the scientific facts on the subject produced to date.
2. That the mental and scholastic achievements of "Negro" children, as with white children, are, in the main, a direct function of their environmental and school opportunities rather than a function of some inherent difference in mental ability.

3. That a philosophy of education based upon the current unwarranted interpretations of achievement differences between white and "Negro" children, as due to inherent racial mental inferiority of the "Negro," is not only UNJUST, but a little short of disastrous, especially in view of the many other disabilities the "Negro" has to undergo in this country. (Thompson, 1928, p. 208)

Along with Horace Mann Bond, Charles H. Thompson placed an uncompromising stake in the ground: he would not accept, in any way, the tenet that blacks were by birth intellectually inferior to whites. Even though he functioned within an academic orthodoxy that accepted this tenet in the mainstream, he would not do so. As more African Americans obtained the level of education required to counter the hereditarians in the scholarly arena, the ranks of the social factors authors would steadily increase.

Albert Sydney Beckham (1897-1964) was a Jay Gould Fellow in psychology at New York University (NYU) in the early 1920s, and he became an assistant professor of psychology at Howard in 1925. Beckham is credited with founding the first psychology laboratory at a black college, but it appears from school archives that Francis Sumner of West Virginia State College already had such a lab in operation by 1925 (Spencer, 1992). In 1928, Beckham began doctoral work at NYU, which he completed in 1930. Robert Daniel (1902-1968), another black scholar in educational psychology, completed his master's degree from Columbia in 1928, subsequently beginning his doctoral work, which he would complete in 1932. He later held the presidency at both Shaw University and Virginia State College.

In 1933, Inez Beverly Prosser (1897-1934) was the first black female to receive a doctorate in educational psychology, which was awarded by the University of Cincinnati. Earlier in the 1920s, she earned a master's degree in educational psychology from the University of Colorado. Prosser was known for her administrative and organizational skills. She held both administrative and academic roles at both Tougaloo College in Mississippi and Tillotson College, a black College in Austin, Texas. She was instrumental in helping African Americans gain an education. Her scholarly career, however, was cut short by a fatal car accident one year after receiving her doctorate.

Howard Hale Long (1888-1948) was a student of G. Stanley Hall (as were Lewis Terman and Francis Sumner, the first black Ph.D. in psychology) at Clark University, where he received a master's degree in experimental psychology in 1916. He worked as a professional in the field for a number of years, and in the late 1920s began work toward his doctorate at Harvard, which he completed in 1933. Long worked as a principal in the Washington D. C. schools from 1925 until 1948. It was in this capacity he worked with Howard University's Bureau of Educational Research, which conducted numerous studies on black students and intelligence assessment in the 1930s and 1940s.

There were a host of other black scholars in psychology finishing up their training and entering the field at the close of the 1920s, but the social factors literature, in particular the literature on the intellectual assessment of African Americans, would have to wait until the 1930s for the emergence of two of the most important writers in that peculiar area: Martin David Jenkins (1904-1978) and Herman George Canady (1901-1970). With the emergence of a considerable number (though still small in absolute terms) of well-trained black scholars, the stage was now set for a torrent of well-designed, well thought-out work that would seriously challenge the claims of the hereditarians.

THE 1930S AND THE EMERGENCE OF A SOCIAL FACTORS PERSPECTIVE

There were now black scholars to compliment the white scholars like Otto Klineberg and Walter Lippman, who took issue with some of the weak points of the hereditarians. Most of the hereditarian literature of this period used the Army Mental Tests as a reference point, while some relied on the Army data quite heavily. However, there were salient problems with the administration of the Army tests, and these problems were glaring targets for those who would seek to assert that there was no provable intellectual superiority of whites over blacks. First, the Army testers, more often than not, failed to follow the research protocol Yerkes established for them. The sheer magnitude of trying to administer tests to 1.7 million men simply made it impossible. Second, African Americans who failed the Alpha test were seldom given the Beta, as Yerkes had intended. Third, those who failed the Beta were to be given an individual test, but the number of illiterate recruits was far greater than Yerkes had predicted, and giving individual examinations to all those who needed them proved impossible. So the validity of the Army Mental Test data was questionable based on its own research criteria. In addition to the problematic administration, Yerkes all but ignored the appreciable correlation of +.75- reported in his own data, between level of education and performance on the tests (Yerkes, 1921, pp. 708-783), and the findings that the scores of northerners, both white and black, were consistently higher than those of southerners. If intelligence were fixed and driven by "race," then southern whites should score similarly to northern whites. They did not. Nor did southern blacks score similarly to northern blacks. The scores of the northern blacks were almost always higher. And there was still the issue of the Army Mental Test concluding that the mental age of the average American was thirteen (Lippman had challenged this position with simple arithmetic and common sense). There were many issues that the proponents of an environmental explanation for intelligence (the social factors people) could use as support of their position.

W. E. B. Du Bois (1868-1963), the world class black scholar whose fields of specialization were neither education nor psychology, but philosophy and sociology, wrote a poignant essay in 1928 that presented a stark and direct challenge to what he considered existing social fallacies. Du Bois wrote:

> In our present discussion of the relations between white and black races in the United States, we are facing an astonishing paradox...the increasing dictum of science is that there are no "races," in any exact scientific sense; ...all present mankind, the world over, are "mixed" so far as the so-called racial characteristics are concerned. (Du Bois, 1928, p. 6)

Du Bois went on to state that a country that continues to support a position unsubstantiated by science, runs the risk of developing a nation of "fools and hypocrites" (p. 6), and that the "racial problem" could be solved by education. As a glaring exception to the general proposition that the "Negro" is the intellectual inferior to the white, Du Bois was one of the reigning intellects of his day. However, if we in the 21st century are to view Du Bois' apparent progressive thinking through a contemporary socio-cultural lens, we would be less than accurate to overlook the fact that Du Bois himself was a staunch believer in the parsimonious distribution of intellectual prowess through access to educational training. His view was that African Americans would be saved by training the "Talented Tenth" among them— who would become the leaders of the race (Du Bois, 1903). Du Bois' observations nonetheless helped to provide a context in which to contest the proclamation of absolute white supremacy. The literature that was to emerge in the 1930s would fill up this context to the extent that, at least from a scholarly standpoint, hereditarianism would be on its heels in defense.

THE JOURNAL OF NEGRO EDUCATION

In 1932, the *Journal of Negro Education* was founded at Howard University to provide a forum for the growing body of research conducted by scholars from the best schools in the country that clearly leaned toward a social factors explanation for performance on intelligence tests. In the inaugural issue, Charles H. Thompson, Senior Editor of the *Journal,* outlined its purpose in an editorial:

> The purpose of the JOURNAL OF NEGRO EDUCATION is three-fold: first, to stimulate the collection, and facilitate the dissemination of facts about the education of Negroes; second, to present discussions involving critical appraisals of the proposals and practices relating to the education of Negroes; and, third, to stimulate and sponsor investigations of problems incident to the education of Negroes. (Thompson, 1932, p. 4)

Thompson went on to explain in careful detail why it was essential not just for African Americans, but also for American society as a whole, that such a journal be started. He explained that there was actually no systematic research being done on the education of blacks in America. There were scattered, sporadic studies at universities here and there, but his office at Howard had received numerous requests for data from other research universities (as did Hampton Institute and Tuskegee). Thompson was also very dissatisfied with the lack of a "critical investigation and thinking" concerning the "assumptions underlying certain basic procedures" in how research involving blacks was undertaken (Thompson, 1932, p. 2). As evidenced in his earlier work, Thompson readily dismissed the idea that African Americans were born inferior, in any way, to whites.

The *Journal* was to be edited and published under the auspices of Howard University and the faculty of the College of Education. The College of Education had just been authorized to organize a "Bureau of Educational Research" which would fund, find funding for, and author research specifically on black education — much of it focused on intelligence assessment. Thompson commented with pride that Howard's College of Education contained the single largest group of professionally trained blacks in education in the country. Accordingly, they were uniquely qualified for the task. However, Thompson was also clear that he did not consider the *Journal* a local enterprise. He wanted input from wherever issues of relevance were occurring, and expected no less than a worldwide audience. The *Journal* was to contain four sections: one for editorial content, another for articles between 3,000 to 3,500 words, a third would deal with reviews of current or past literature, and a fourth would address current events.

The *Journal of Negro Education* took little time to get up to speed. The first edition contained articles from Horace Mann Bond and W. E. B. Du Bois, and immediately began to address the claim of white intellectual superiority with an article by Alice McAlpin entitled, "Changes in the Intelligence Quotients of Negro Children" (McAlpin, 1932). In this article, McAlpin provided something that most of the hereditarians had ignored (harkening the readers' attention to Thompson's comment on the need for a *Journal* such as his), and even the social factors researchers had touched upon intermittently, intra-race analysis. Intra-race analysis would be more the rule than the exception of the articles generated by black scholars in the area of intelligence assessment.

McAlpin gave all of the children in the 3A and 5A grades of the colored schools in the District of Columbia the Kuhlmann-Anderson test (see Shuey, 1958) to determine how the IQ averages of the pupils varied with length of residence in the District. The 3A children born in the District had an average IQ of 98.1. The 3A children born outside the District had an average IQ of 92.1. Of those 5A children born in the District, the median IQ was 95.1, while that of the 5A children born outside the District was 89.7. The higher median IQ for the children born in the District, McAlpin contended, was due to the favorable environment enjoyed there. This article brought to light the within-group differences that were clearly attributable to exposure to better educational opportunity. While there were certainly other possible explanations for the improvement in test scores, the relationship between having a quality education and higher performance was unmistakable. And numerous researchers would attain similar results in the years to come.

In another article in this inaugural edition of the *Journal,* Maudelle B. Bousfield observed a consistent, but not overwhelming relationship between poverty and poor intelligence test performance in a group of Chicago students ranging from grade 5 to 8 (Bousfield, 1932). And in many studies by Martin Jenkins and other Howard University researchers, intra-race analysis would offer many interesting findings.

It did not take long for people to see the tremendous benefit of the *Journal of Negro Education.* In October of 1932, in the *Journal's* third issue, Howard Hale Long, the brilliant, Harvard-trained educational researcher, provided a piercing book review of Myrtle McGraw's work, *A Comparison of Negro and White Infants* (McGraw, 1931). McGraw's contention was that there existed developmental differences between white and black children that could be detected within the first year of birth. She developed a scale called the "development quotient" (much along the lines of IQ, the construct earlier developed by Lewis Terman that was supposed to be the quotient mental age/chronological age) that showed a clear superiority of white children. Howard H. Long methodically dismantled McGraw's argument in a variety of ways. His quantitative training at Harvard was as rigorous as anywhere in the world, and he cited flaw after flaw in McGraw's statistical analyses (Long, 1932). While it is possible that other scholarly journals would have detected the shortcomings of what Long said was, overall, a worthy effort by McGraw, making such observations was the *rasion d'etre* of the *Journal of Negro Education*. Now there existed a group of well-trained, intellectually vigorous scholars to challenge the flawed contributions in the literature on black intelligence. The hereditarians could no longer make vague, unsubstantiated claims, as they had been able to do until the late 1920s, without the existence of a critical force to take them to task.

Book reviews were to play a salient role in how the *Journal of Negro Education* fulfilled its mission. Because a good portion of American education was segregated (it was almost totally segregated in the South), and because this segregation facilitated a skewered view of the intelligence of African Americans, it was imperative that literature pertaining to race and intelligence, or race and education, be subjected to a critical analysis. This was analysis the *Journal* was more than willing to provide. It made its objective clear on the first page of its "Current Literature on Negro Education" section:

> The general purpose of this division of the Journal is the announcement, description, and critical review of current literature dealing *directly* or *indirectly* [italics the author's] with various phases of the education of Negroes. It is designed to be the unique and reliable source to which those seeking such material may have regular recourse. (Editor, 1934, p. 3)

Given the stature of the reviewers, the book reviews in the *Journal of Negro Education* would be taken seriously. Joseph St. Clair Price, who would later become the Dean of the College of Liberal Arts at Howard, contributed several such reviews. In January of 1933, Price reviewed Thomas Garth's *Race and Psychology in America* (Garth, 1931). Price gave Garth a favorable review for his stance— that he (Garth) saw no substantiation for ascribing differences in performance on intelligence tests solely to the race of the examinee. Price presented Garth's declaration that purely racial comparisons of intelligence were virtually impossible unless: 1) the term "race" could be rigidly defined, and a truly representative sample be used; 2) the races must have equal access to education; and 3) the measurements be valid for both racial groups (Price, 1933a). Price also commended Garth for his pointing out that ascribing inherited psychological characteristics to the racial group the subject belonged to was untenable, because there was no proof that those cognitive characteristics were peculiar to a specific race. However, Price's review of Garth's book was far from entirely complimentary. He chided it for being too light on facts and not focused enough specifically on intelligence measurement.

Another review by Joseph St. Clair Price addressed Clark Foreman's *Environmental Factors in Negro Elementary Education* (Foreman, 1932). Here we have an example of the high literary standards of the *Journal*. Foreman's work, according to Price, clearly and concisely demonstrated that as social factors for African Americans improved, so did their test scores. However, even though Foreman's thesis was one that was supported by the *Journal,* Price was still unyielding in his critique of Foreman's method. "One wonders, though, whether this problem of the measurement of racial mental differences is quite so simple. Such investigators as Garth, Klineberg, and even Peterson do not seem to consider it so" (Price, 1933b, p. 508). This monograph was part of Foreman's dissertation at Columbia. Price, and the *Journal*, could have let his statements stand unqualified as further evidence of the fallacy of racial superiority. Instead, Price gave a detailed critique not only of Foreman's facts, but of his prose style of writing as well, "To the busy or impartial reader the work would be both disappointing and provoking because of its very poor organization and its homely style" (p. 509). One would have to do more than just refute the tenets of racial superiority to receive a laudatory review in the *Journal*; one would also have to craft one's prose skillfully and provide an acceptable research methodology.

However, providing a critique of literary style was far from the main purpose of the *Journal's* reviewers. As demonstrated by my earlier mention of a review by H. H. Long, the *Journal* prided itself on the quantitative acumen of its reviewers. Long provided another review in January of 1934; this time it was a review of Raymond Clark's doctoral dissertation, *The Effect of Schooling Upon the Intelligence Quotients of Negro Children* (Clark, 1933). Clark's thesis, in analyzing data from 1,256 black students in Cleveland and Detroit, was that a northern education would do little to boost the IQs of southern-born blacks. He provided data that attested to the fact that after a period of time in northern schools, the IQs of the southern-born blacks improved little. Long gently pointed out that Raymond had, perhaps, applied the wrong formula to compute the standard error of the differences between the mean scores, and perhaps, more importantly, the author was apparently unaware that numerous researchers, as far back as Arlitt (1922), claimed that they found a consistent decrease in African Americans' IQ as age increased. Further still, Long chided the author for failing to include a control group of the same age that remained in the South. Had the IQs of both the southern and northern blacks remained unchanged overtime then, Clark would have had a stronger substantiation for his case. As it stood, how was Clark to know that the northern education had not *prevented* the deterioration of the southern-born blacks' IQs, as much previous data had indicated we could expect (Long, 1934)?

While it was not explicitly about intelligence measurement, Charles H. Thompson's review of Horace Mann Bond's *The Education of the Negro in the American Social Order* (1934) warrants some mention. While Thompson's review was not an unmitigated accolade, it was praise enough for one of the most important works on black education ever written. Here is an example of the *Journal* in its finest form. Thompson, one of the esteemed researchers who comprised the vanguard of the black intellectual future, offered a sober, mature critique of another- younger- intellectual giant. Thompson was careful in his praise. He was critical about the organization of Bond's book, arguing that it would be "confusing" to a non-scholar. Nevertheless, Thompson's pride in Bond's work was unmistakable. Thompson concluded his review by stating: "This volume not only presents the most complete summary of the main facts concerning Negro education now available, but explains them in a very engaging and lucid style" (Thompson, 1935, p. 269). For reviewers to whom style was almost as important as substance, this was glowing praise, indeed.

In 1935, J. S. Price reviewed Otto Klineberg's *Negro Intelligence and Selective Migration* (Klineberg, 1935). Klineberg authored a work that would attack one of the pillars of the hereditarian argument: that the test scores of northern blacks were consistently higher only because the more educated blacks ("smarter") migrated to the North— otherwise known as the "Selective Migration Hypothesis." At the beginning of his review, Price methodically identified the three camps of the argument as they existed in his day. One was the hereditarians (Price used this word explicitly) who pointed to the differences in test scores on the Army tests as solid proof of a genetic difference between the intellects of blacks and whites. Price placed Carl C. Brigham (Brigham, 1923) and George O. Ferguson (Ferguson, 1921) in this group. A second group into which Price placed himself, H. H. Long, and

Charles H. Thompson consisted of investigators who created no new studies, but spent considerable time pouring over the existing data. A third group, which Price called the experimental investigators, engaged in controlled studies that sought to understand the nature of the perceived differences between the races. In this group, Price placed Arlitt, Garth, and Klineberg. It is within this framework that Price reviews Klineberg's work (Price, 1935).

Klineberg's overall thesis was that not only were there no supporting data for the selective migration hypothesis, but there were ample data to directly contradict it. For example, Klineberg obtained the school records of 562 children from Birmingham, Alabama; Charleston, South Carolina; and Nashville, Tennessee who migrated either to a northern city, another city in the South, or a rural area in the South. Klineberg detected no difference in the school performance of the migrants versus the entire population. Next, Klineberg performed a detailed analysis, utilizing a variety of commonly used intelligence tests (e.g., Otis, Stanford-Binet, etc.) on 3,081 ten and twelve year old African American boys and girls who migrated to New York City from the South (his study included a control group of New York born African Americans of the same age). He found a significant and consistent correlation between the length of time a subject lived in New York and their test performance.

As always, no author, not even one as well respected as Klineberg, would escape the *Journal's* meticulous analysis. Giving no consideration to Klineberg's esteem as a scholar, Price was quick to point out that in some of the testing, the sample sizes were too small to warrant the emphasis Klineberg placed on the results (some of the Stanford-Binet tests that were administered, had as few as 40 subjects). Nevertheless, overall, Price and the *Journal* were quite pleased with Klineberg's work as a landmark study.

MORE SOCIAL FACTORS LITERATURE IN THE 1930S

All of the social factors literature of the 1930s was not presented in the *Journal of Negro Education*—just a good portion of it. Albert Sydney Beckham (1897-1964), who in 1930 received his Ph.D. from New York University, in 1933, he wrote an article in the *Journal of Social Psychology* in which he sought to determine the effect of environment on IQ scores (curiously, Beckham repeatedly referred to Dagny Sunne as "he" in the article) (Beckham, 1933). Using the Taussig measure of socioeconomic status (see Shuey, 1958) and the Stanford-Binet as a measure of intelligence, Beckham found what numerous others found and would find in the future: social factors had a clear influence on intelligence test performance. In his observation of black adolescents from New York, Washington, the District of Columbia, and Baltimore, Maryland, Beckham found that the students from New York clearly did better than the students from the other two cities, and that the students from higher socioeconomic status environments clearly and consistently did better than those from poorer backgrounds.

There was still a lot of rich literature that was yet to come out of the *Journal of Negro Education*. In 1934, the *Journal* published an edition entitled, "The Physical and Mental Abilities of the Negro." In it was a stunning compilation of articles focused on the status of the intellectual assessment of African Americans. It contained articles by Robert P. Daniel, Frank N. Freeman, Thomas Garth, Mellville Herskovits, Charles S. Johnson and Horace Mann Bond, Robert Pintner, C. E. Smith, Doxey A. Wilkerson, Paul Witty and Martin Jenkins, Otto Klineberg, Joseph Peterson, Joseph St. Clair Price, Walter Dearborn and Howard Long, and Editor in Chief, Charles H. Thompson. It was an awesome display of the intellectual power of the *Journal*. Most of the authors, many of whom had no direct connection with Howard or the *Journal* at all, were acknowledged as being at the top of their field. It was truly a landmark, not only for the *Journal of Negro Education,* but for the field of intellectual assessment, especially as it pertained to African Americans. The *Journal* appeared to have reached a new level of maturity and objectivity.

Melville J. Herskovits (1895-1963), the highly acclaimed cultural anthropologist (and student of Franz Boas), provided a lengthy discussion on the "Mulatto Hypothesis." Much like Klineberg, Herskovits claimed there was no substantiation for the theory, but he approached the problem as an anthropologist rather than a psychologist. Herskovits was meticulous in an aspect that many, if not most, of the researchers in racial comparisons were not trying to develop: a clear understanding of the term "race." Herskovits may not have arrived at a definition of race, but he offered a serious and determined effort to do so. He started out by establishing the nature of the human race, "… mankind must be regarded as comprising one species of the biological series" (Herskovits, 1934, p. 392). He continues, "The fact that a population is classified by students as belonging to a given race may be useful as well as interesting; it may, furthermore, be a fact of enormous social importance; biologically, however, it explains nothing" (p. 393). This was coming not from the ranks of psychological or educational researchers, who could be and often were unclear about something as nebulous as race; it was coming from a cultural anthropologist at the top of his field, to whom an understanding of the concept of race was an essential matter. If Herskovits was right, and all subsequent genetic findings have supported his position completely, then the argument about a genetically inferior "race" had no legs to stand on. While it certainly was within the realm of possibility for intelligence to be inherited from one's parents, it was impossible to derive a genetically based intellectual benefit from belonging to a given race if the concept of race itself had no genetic basis.

Klineberg, who was steadily gaining momentum and reputation as a debunker of the belief in purely racial intellectual differences, followed up where Herskovits left off. In his article, he provided a basis for viewing intelligence as a function of the social context. He points to basic semantic differences that vary from one cultural context to another when applied to a simple word like "school" (Klineberg, 1934, p. 479), and the different perceptions of the importance of completing certain tasks (like the completion of an intelligence assessment). "When the cultural differences are great, the tests so far developed may be entirely inapplicable. In extreme cases, even the competitive attitude, which test performance almost invariably presupposes, may be entirely lacking" (p. 478). We can even see the beginnings of a challenge to the construct of intelligence itself (something that was not common in the psychological literature of the era) when Klineberg places the term *intelligence* in quotes when describing it on page 483.

The rest of the articles in this landmark edition were more of the same: reinforcement of the findings of intra-race studies in terms of the variability of IQ among African Americans of different socioeconomic status (Long, 1934), which created weaknesses in the arguments of the hereditarians (Price, 1934). One article, in particular, deserves special mention. Charles H. Thompson (Thompson, 1934) contributed "The Conclusion of Scientists Relative to Racial Differences" in this issue. It was a comprehensive overview of the perceptions of 169 of the leading psychologists, educational researchers (whom Thompson calls "educationists"), sociologists, and anthropologists (who Thompson lumped together in one group) of the day in the area of intelligence assessment (Thompson, 1934). Thompson compiled a list of questions concerning various aspects of the mental measurements of African Americans. He placed these questions into a survey and mailed them to leading scholars in the aforementioned three areas. The list of respondents to the survey was impressive. It included: Ada Arlitt, Edwin Boring (who had worked with Yerkes on the Army Mental Tests), Carl Brigham, Thomas Garth, Jean Piaget, Joseph Peterson, Lewis Terman, and Robert Yerkes from psychology, among many others. From education, there was John Dewey and W.C. Bagley from Columbia, and representatives from the University of Chicago, Ohio State, New York University, and Harvard, but there were also participants from the University of Alabama, the University of Kentucky, and Louisiana State University. From the fields of sociology and anthropology, there was Franz Boas of Columbia, E. W. Burgess and Fay Cooper-Cole from the University of Chicago, Loomis Havemeyer from Yale, and J. H. Sellin, F. G. Speck and Donald Young from the University of Pennsylvania. It was clearly a scholarly group. It might be noted also, that there was not one representative from a black college among the respondents. All in all, Thompson had responses from 100 psychologists, 30 educationists, and 39 sociologists and anthropologists.

Thompson began by presenting a framework offered by Dale Yoder (1901-1990) of the University of Minnesota (Yoder, 1928), which identified three distinct viewpoints for the existing literature on racial intellectual differences: 1) an acceptance of the claim of racial superiority and inferiority and an interest in re-stating this fact, usually adducing additional evidence to support the thesis, 2) that the existence of racial superiority is possible, but not adequately supported by existing data- this viewpoint balanced arguments for and against the idea, and 3) a skeptical position which was highly critical of the means used to demonstrate race inferiority and of the results which supported it (Thompson, 1934, p. 498).

Thompson stated that 72% of his respondents agreed with Yoder's framework as valid, and 28% felt it was not representative. However, when Thompson provided a breakdown by discipline, of the parts of Yoder's proposition that the scholars agreed with the most, the differences were interesting. A majority of the psychologists (54%) felt that Yoder's second position— that racial inferiority was possible, but not completely established by the data, was valid, while 44% of the educationists and only 20% of the sociologists and anthropologists felt this claim was supported by the research. Some 65% of the sociologists and anthropologists felt that Yoder's third position – that the evidence of racial inferiority was questionable in nature, was valid. Admittedly, there were decidedly fewer sociologists and anthropologists, but throughout the survey, the responses of both the educationists and the sociologists and anthropologists were consistently more inclined to doubt that the evidence proved racial superiority than were the psychologists. For example, on the question of whether the existing data from recent investigations proved the inferiority of African Americans, grouped together only 10% of both the educationists and sociologists/anthropologists felt it did, while a full 25% of the psychologists believed it did. And 25% of the educationists and sociologists/anthropologists (grouped together) felt that the data indicated that blacks were equal to whites in terms of inherent mental ability, while only 11% of the psychologists did (Thompson, 1934, p. 499).

Probably the most revealing difference in how the groups perceived the question of racial comparisons was how they answered the question on the "Mulatto Hypothesis." While their responses to whether the data were inconclusive were close (68% of the psychologists felt they were, while 65% of the educationists and 76% of the sociologists/anthropologists did), none of the sociologists/anthropologists felt the data supported the racial superiority claim. Approximately 25% of both the two non-psychology groups felt the data refuted it, while only 9% of the psychologists felt the same (Thompson, 1934, p. 507).

It should be noted that the composition of the respondents was far from random; there were many more southern universities represented among the psychologists and educationists than there were among the sociologists and anthropologists. It was clear that of the group under discussion, the non-psychologists were considerably more skeptical of the data than were the psychologists. And the sociologists/anthropologists unanimously rejected the "Mulatto Hypothesis" as not being supported by the evidence. This hypothesis was one of the foundations of the hereditarian position. If it were true that lighter complexioned blacks scored higher on intelligence tests because they had more "white blood," the validity of racial superiority in terms of intellect would be much more reinforced. But if not, and lighter complexioned blacks scored higher on the tests because of better social advantages, then the case was made weaker. From an expertise standpoint, it certainly stood to reason that in terms of a complex social phenomenon like race (and many anthropologists, like Melville Herskovits, saw race as just that), sociologists and anthropologists were more competent to make such determinations than were psychologists.

Thompson's article, along with the works of Klineberg and Melville Herskovits, constituted something of a *coup de grace* against the two pillars of the hereditarians' argument of racial superiority— the "Mulatto Hypothesis" and selective migration. If neither of these positions could be supported, then the concept of racial superiority would be brought seriously into question. If racial superiority were brought into question, then the theory of the inheritability of intelligence was weakened (though not necessarily disproved). If the theory of the inheritability of intelligence was weakened, then the way was opened for a clearer (and more applicable) theory regarding the nature of intelligence itself. While all of this was not the direct result of Thompson's effort, those of us who now view human intellectual activity as a fundamentally social phenomenon, can point to it as a theoretical watershed.

In the 1930s, Martin D. Jenkins and Herman Canady emerged as two prominent scholars of exceptional skill and vision who would have a permanent impact on both American psychology and American education. For all of their boldness in taking on the intellectual *status quo* of their time, writers like Lippman, Herskovits, and Klineberg were white middle class researchers. In the 1930s, there were places that a white person, even a white Jew (all three researchers were Jewish), could venture to in American society where a black person could not. During the 1930s, there began to emerge a cadre of brilliant and bold African American scholars who had some of the finest education America had to offer, and they were ready and willing to challenge some of the nation's most basic beliefs about racial minorities. Martin Jenkins and Herman Canady were among this group.

MARTIN JENKINS

Jenkins was born in 1904 in Terre Haute, Indiana (the same state from which Lewis Terman hailed) into a family of modest means. He attended public school there, graduating from high school in 1921. He then attended Howard University, majoring in mathematics and graduating in 1925. From 1925 until 1930, Jenkins worked with his father in the construction business and attended Indiana State College, obtaining a second bachelor's degree, this one in education.

Jenkins went to teach education at Virginia State College, a black college, in 1930, but obtained a graduate fellowship to Northwestern in 1932, and was awarded a master's degree from there in 1933. Jenkins continued his graduate studies in educational psychology at Northwestern under Paul A. Witty, and was awarded a doctorate in 1935. His dissertation subject, "A Socio-Psychological Study of Negro Children of Superior Intelligence," (1936) set the tone for his career. Many of the studies up to that time claimed that while there was a variance in the intelligence scores of African Americans, it would be an extreme rarity to find blacks with scores as high as the high scores of white students. Jenkins's study clearly demonstrated that while as a group, the scores of African Americans were lower than those of whites, there were many more high scoring blacks than the existing literature would lead one to believe.

Jenkins began by stating that while the "gifted" child (and by reading Jenkins's work it becomes clear that to him a gifted child can be identified via an intelligence test) had been the subject of much study, little attention was given to gifted African Americans. He used a sample of eight thousand black Chicago students from grades 3-8; his selection criteria were similar to those of Terman's earlier studies. The teachers would select children based on the following criteria: students they thought were most intelligent, who were doing the best work, and students who were one or one-and-a-half years above age-grade. This resulted in 539 students (6.5% of the school population). He then applied the McCall Multi-Mental Scale (see Shuey, 1958), a group test. For students who scored over 120 on the McCall scale, he administered the Stanford-Binet, an individual test. Jenkins also used the Sims Score Card for Socio-Economic Status (see Shuey, 1958).

One of the first things to notice about Jenkins' 1935 study is the preponderance of girls. There were 72 girls and 31 boys found with IQs of 120 and above. Jenkins commented that this was clearly at odds with the gender makeup found for such groups in the past. Jenkins also noticed, as would be found by many similar studies in the future, that his high IQ students consistently came from well-educated families. The median educational level of the fathers was 13.9 years, and that for mothers was 12.8 years. Seventy percent of the high IQ students had parents in professional, clerical, or semi-professional fields. This was in line with the findings of Terman and others in earlier studies. He did not, however, find a strong effect of the Sims Scale data on IQ. Jenkins made a distinction between SES and profession/education. This separation of occupation from SES is intriguing, but not unique to Jenkins in this era.

Jenkins concluded his groundbreaking study on African Americans by stating that, "Superior Negro children are not anomalous in the elementary school population" (Jenkins, 1936, p. 189), and "...Negro children are not inherently different from other American children" (p. 190). Thus, there began a theme that would persist through much of Jenkins's work: the black population was not intellectually different from the white population. Jenkins was on a ceaseless quest for the "gifted Negro." It would be easy to criticize Jenkins's acceptance of American psychology's model of intelligence with our 2010 socio-cultural eyes. However, it is unarguable that he demonstrated that he could find many blacks of unquestioned ability, as defined using the accepted tool of IQ, if one looked in places that were unexplored.

In 1936, Jenkins collaborated with his highly respected mentor from Northwestern, Paul Witty, in an article entitled, "Intra-Race Testing and Negro

Intelligence" (Witty and Jenkins, 1936). This study used data from Jenkins' earlier work in Chicago to re-state what had become by 1936 a rather standard refutation of the racial inferiority of blacks, and, in light of the work of Melville Herskovits and Otto Klineberg, an equally routine refutation of the "Mulatto Hypothesis." By the mid-1930s, there was an ever-increasing parade of interdisciplinary data, aided by Herskovits and Boas from anthropology, and numerous writers from education and psychology, which beat a steady cadence of repudiation of the hereditarians.

In 1939, Jenkins added still more fuel to the fire. In "The Mental Ability of the Negro" (Jenkins, 1939). Jenkins somewhat departs from his usual research position of seeing African Americans simply as a variant of mainstream America. Instead, Jenkins argues that, "The position which any group occupies in the social structure at any given time depends upon a complex of variable factors which are historical, sociological, psychological and economic in nature" (p. 511). While his paper does go on to describe intelligence as something inborn and quantifiable, Jenkins acknowledges the probable overwhelming influence of society upon intelligence. In yet another assault upon "racial difference," Jenkins once again meticulously explains the obvious flaws of the racial intelligence comparisons of the past. By 1939, Jenkins and many others had disproved the major tenets of the hereditarian argument many times over, and Jenkins once more used his shopworn Chicago dissertation data to show that African Americans were the intellectual equal of whites, using the same criteria that were used to establish white intellectual superiority.

Jenkins would go on to serve as an administrator at several black colleges. While it is easy to take issue with Jenkins' painless acceptance regarding the mainstream measurement of intelligence, he saw through many of the problems in how this assessment was applied. It was clear to him that environment played a big role in intellectual development, and even using the tools of his day, he found many more "gifted" African Americans than the white researchers did. Later we will see a study by Jenkins that makes it clear that he saw the perils to come in the education of his people.

HERMAN G. CANADY

Of all the psychologists, anthropologists, and educators discussed in this chapter, none so quite fit what I feel is the spirit of the work of Alfred Binet as Herman G. Canady (1901-1970). Canady appears to stand alone among the American psychologists of the 1930s in his detailed analysis regarding the social context of black students' lives, and making every effort to match the educational environment to their needs.

Canady was the son of a poor Methodist minister who had to supplement his small pastor's salary with donations of food and clothing from the congregation. The early twentieth century was a precarious time for a black family of limited means, and Canady's family often had to uproot itself due to the caprice of Jim Crow economics. In spite of his family's harsh circumstances, Herman Canady grew up with a rigid moral code that would sustain him for his entire life (Spencer, 1992).

Canady attended Northwestern University, completing a bachelor's degree in sociology in 1927 and a master's degree in clinical psychology in 1928. Later, he would complete his doctorate in 1941. When it was time to seek an appointment to teach psychology, Canady's prospects were severely limited. Without a Ph.D. his prospects of teaching at a white university were virtually non-existent. And as for black colleges, only Howard and West Virginia State College had actual programs in psychology. Francis Sumner, the student of G. Stanley Hall at Clark University and the first black to be awarded a Ph.D. in psychology, started the program in psychology at West Virginia State. When Sumner came to Howard University in Washington, D. C., this left a job open at West Virginia State. After several exchanges of letters between President John Davis of West Virginia State and Canady, it was decided that he was to come to West Virginia State to head the psychology department. This was in 1928. He would stay at West Virginia State for his entire career.

Immediately, Canady began to observe that the curriculum at West Virginia State was poorly fit to the students there. He wrote to the president in 1929, informing him that he (Canady) had developed instruments to both measure his effectiveness as a teacher and his students' respective strengths and weaknesses (Canady, 1929). This clearly set the tone of Canady's career. He argued that black colleges were obligated to do all they could to best fit their programs to their students' needs.

Canady's major contributions to the literature of psychology and education began in 1935 with the publication of "Individual Differences Among Freshmen at West Virginia State College" (Canady, 1935). In this work, he analyzed the socio-cultural experiences of the students at West Virginia State, and recommended devising appropriate individualized curricula for each student in this context. Canady, a black professor at a black college, defined the role of education quite differently than many of his contemporaries. As was the case with Binet, Canady did not see his role as setting limits upon his students based on test scores. Instead he saw his role as understanding who his students were, where they came from, where they wanted to go, and how to help them get there. Canady pointed out that the variance in SES among the students was great, but the variety in the programs was limited. He proposed setting up an individual program appropriate to each student. While the administration at West Virginia State had the utmost respect for Herman Canady, the record does not show that they acted upon his recommendations to any discernable extent.

In 1936 Canady published his master's thesis, "The Effect of 'Rapport' on the IQ: A New Approach to the Problem of Racial Psychology" (Canady, 1936a). His intention was to show that performance on IQ tests was affected by the race of the examiner. He was successful to an extent. His results, though significant, were also erratic. It appeared that rapport between examiner and subject was a factor in IQ test performance, but this was not clearly demonstrated.

With the publication of "The Intelligence of Negro College Students and Parental Occupation" (Canady, 1936b), it was obvious Canady found his calling and his niche. In this particular study, Canady showed with clear logic and precise design the relationship between socio-economic status and performance on intelligence assessments. Some hereditarians had noticed that the relationship between occupation and IQ scores was not perfect. Canady acknowledged this, but went on to demonstrate that this was due to observable within-group individual differences (that is, within-group variance) and that, overall, the relationship between SES and IQ was fairly consistent. It is his detailed analysis of intra-race data that gives Canady's work its power, and makes it distinct among American psychologists, including Klineberg and Jenkins, for developing a socio-cultural perspective on intelligence.

In 1938, Canady published a study on the state of departments of psychology in black colleges (Canady, 1938b), which he said were virtually non-existent. In addition, he conducted another study on gender differences among the students at West Virginia State (Canady, 1938a). Though psychological research among black universities in general may have been lacking in the 1930s, the remotely located West Virginia State, with Canady as the driving force, could be viewed as a center of psychological research on

African Americans. A great deal of quality work came out of Howard University also, but most of it was being conducted by scholars in education and not psychology per se (even though Canady did not get his doctorate in psychology until 1941, when he did, he was still one of only a handful of blacks with this credential). The West Virginia State Research Council convened in 1937 with the specific purpose of identifying and supporting quality research about African Americans. Their portfolio of projects, led by the work of Herman Canady, is still impressive.

1940-1945

The close of the 1930s left the literature with a rich repository of information that presented a sweeping refutation of hereditarianism. With Klineberg, Jenkins, Canady, and the Howard University group leading the way, and with support from the disciplines of anthropology and sociology that buttressed the social factors case, we have been left with a substantial foundation for a socio-cultural perspective of intelligence.

In 1940, it was clear to many that America's participation in World War II would be inevitable. Herein lies a dilemma: One of the major tenets of Nazi Germany was the inherent superiority claim of the Aryan "race" above all others. There was a similar belief system at work in the United States. One of the most fundamental premises of the American philosophy was the inherent and unchangeable superiority of whites over blacks. This was a premise that was firmly supported by custom, law, and social policy. It was also firmly supported by many in the social sciences. American psychology was, it appeared, mired in the belief of a racial intellectual hierarchy, no matter how little scientific support for this belief existed or how much evidence against it was presented. Robert Yerkes, Lewis Terman, Henry Goddard, and Carl Brigham had all built luminary careers based on this hierarchy, although with the exception of Yerkes, all would, in one way or another, eventually make public retractions of their earlier positions. For whatever reason, the mainstream of American psychology appeared convinced of three things: 1) that intelligence was something that could be accurately quantified; 2) that one was born with a fixed amount of intelligence, and 3) race was a factor in the level of intelligence with which one was born. By 1940, the next generation of hereditarians was emerging, Hans Eysenck, for example, who would carry on the belief in inheritable intelligence. However, the social factors writers were far from finished.

In January of 1940, Fay-Cooper Cole, the illustrious anthropologist who is known for creating the department of anthropology at the University of Chicago in 1929 (and was one of the respondents to Charles H. Thompson's survey on racial psychology in the 1930s), wrote an important article in *The American Teacher* titled, "An Anthropologist's View on Race" (Cole, 1940). This article was less inspired by the inaccuracies of "racial psychology" than it was by the emerging anti-Semitism in Europe (and, probably to a lesser extent, in America, too). Its relevance to the arguments raised by the hereditarians is clear. Race, as the term was being misused at the time of Cole's writing, had nothing to do with intelligence. In fact, race had little to do with anything other than the pseudo-importance a society may choose to give it arbitrarily. This was said before, of course, by Boas, Klineberg, Herskovits, and many others. However, that was in a somewhat different social climate. Now America would be asking its sons and daughters to offer up their lives for a set of ideals. The debate among the scholarly community was that: Just what did those ideals represent?

Between 1942 and 1943, Herman Canady made several contributions that can be considered significant. In January of 1942, Canady and two colleagues published a scale to assess the stimulation level of the home environment of black youth (Canady et al., 1942a). Canady, being something of a socio-cultural theorist before there ever was such a creation, was convinced that not only could intelligence be explained and analyzed via the social context, but that it was the social context that would layout a roadmap illustrating how to best educate our students. It bears repeating continuously: this is precisely the approach Binet felt would be most effective, and Canady, as far as I can determine, is the only major American psychologist of his time to so closely mirror Binet's approach. He felt that a special scale was needed for black students. It is apparent from his personal notes that he believed that all students would benefit from such a specialized approach to testing, not just African Americans. Canady argued that the Sims Score Card (the prevailing measure of SES during Canady's day) lacked the granularity needed to capture the differences between the social conditions of African Americans and whites. He believed that a given social parameter, like income, would not convey the same information in differing social contexts.

Canady's scale for black youth was developed by ten judges. These included five black experts in anthropology, education, and psychology, and five white professors from the psychology and education departments at Northwestern. Of this effort Canady argued, "An attempt was made to evaluate the whole complex of psychological conditions that may impinge directly or indirectly on the intellectual development of Negro youth" (Canady, 1942, p. 4). This was not merely accepting and using parameters that white society deemed good measures of the social context for everyone, blacks included. Rather, this was building the measurement criteria from the ground up to ensure that they were appropriate for the social context in question, namely that of African American youth. It included items such as social contacts, extra-curricular activities, social and cultural level of the community (which included the level of racial segregation of the community), and parental attitude toward education.

The correlation between Canady's Environmental Scale and the Sims SES test was reported as .73 ± .04. The Sims' Score Card for Socio-Economic Status gathered data on factors such as parental occupation, schooling, rooms per house, and number of books in the home. It was used as a standard measure of socio-economic status in the 1930s and 1940s (Sims, 1921). The correlation between the Sims SES test and intelligence test score (among the West Virginia State students) was .16 ± .06, and the correlation of coefficient between Canady's Environmental Scale and the intelligence test scores for the West Virginia State students was .32 ± .05. While this last figure is not as high as one might think it should be, it is still almost double that of the correlation between the Sims test and the West Virginia State student scores, indicating obvious value in a more precise measure of a students' social situation. Canady was careful to point out that his scale had the same reliability coefficient as the Sims test (91). He also clearly differentiated his scale from the Sims test. The Sims test was purely an economic and material measure of family possessions. Canady said that was important but incomplete. What was more important, he argued, was how many plays the family attended, how much they traveled, and what possibilities did the family hold as being realistic for its offspring?

In March of 1942, he published yet another article that used his now voluminous data on the students at West Virginia State to indicate the effect of socio-economic status on intelligence test performance (this time using the more widely accepted Sims SES scale rather than his own) (Canady, 1942). Of interest in this article is Canady's assault on the Americanized concept of "race." Canady placed the term in quotes whenever he used it in the article. He cited Herskovits and others in stating that race in America is a social rather than a biological or anthropological term. In another article in *School and Society* in May of 1942, with a war against racial supremacy raging in Europe, Canady examined the fallacy in the method employed in intelligence testing (Canady, 1942). He pointed to the Paul Young study at Louisiana State

University in the 1920s (Young, 1929), among others, as particularly bad examples of how to conduct such research. Canady continued along this vein in a more scholarly fashion in a 1943 article in which he argues that any intellectual comparison between whites and blacks, using the then prevailing approaches, was invalid because of the completely different social circumstances of the two groups (Canady, 1943a). He once again returned to his valuable West Virginia State student data, but this time to see if there were gender differences. He concluded that at least among his students, overall performance and variability were the same among males and females, but in specific areas there appeared to be a gender effect that was indeterminate in nature. In some subjects, the females did consistently better than the males, in others consistently poorer (Canady, 1943b). Herman Canady would continue to contribute to the literature for another 25 years.

Similarly, Martin Jenkins continued his work with one of his better known studies: "Case Studies of Negro Children of Binet IQ 160 and Above" (Jenkins, 1943). As was invariably the case, Jenkins observed that his gifted African Americans came from "high socio-economic status homes" (p. 163). Be that as it may, one wonders whether these students would have been identified as gifted were it not for the work of Jenkins and Witty.

As if to staunch the assault on the deluge of social factors literature in the 1940s, Alper and Boring (Yerkes's assistant on the Army Mental Tests project) published an article in 1944 entitled, "Intelligence-Test Scores of Northern and Southern White and Negro Recruits in 1918" (Alper and Boring, 1944). In it, they acknowledge that, yes, northern blacks scored much higher than southern blacks on the Army tests. This, they allowed, could have been attributable to a higher level of education. But they were critical of Klineberg's analysis, and said it did not give an accurate presentation of the data. Alper and Boring claimed that, in fact, *skin color,* along with geography, were factors on how well a subject performed on the Army Mental Tests. They attempted to support this position with a different analysis of the Army Mental Tests, which sought to calculate the separate effects of "skin color" (which is merely another term Alper and Boring use for race), geography (North or South), and any interaction between the two factors (Alper and Boring, 1944, p. 473). Their claim was that after accounting for geographical differences, skin color was still a salient factor in intelligence.

Just as with the initial Army data, the data for Alper and Boring's 1944 study are confusing. On page 472 they state that, "Beta was given to all men who scored low on Alpha, because either they were stupid or unable to read English." This, according to notes by Yerkes himself, subsequent to the administration of the Army tests in 1918 – was not true. Because of the overwhelming number of subjects involved, uncounted numbers of African Americans who failed the Alpha and were supposed to be given the Beta, did not have the Beta administered to them. In Yerkes's own monograph he states that:

> The very large percentage of Negroes too illiterate to take alpha placed a special emphasis upon the question of the suitability of beta as a test for these subjects. Opinions of examiners differ somewhat on this question, but the general consensus seems to be that the beta is not as satisfactory a test for illiterate Negro recruits as it is for illiterate whites. (Yerkes, 1921, p. 705)

As with every other effort that sought to redeem some validity for the Army Mental Test data, Alper and Boring were contradicted by the sheer confusion of the tests' data. Not only was the research protocol too seldom followed, Yerkes himself questioned the worth of the tests when used to compare whites and blacks.

In yet another illustrative piece of writing, Jenkins, in his role as a senior researcher at Howard's Bureau of Educational Research, authored a report to the Committee on Current Educational Problems of Negroes (Jenkins, 1945). The report was a summation of the results on a series of standardized tests given to schoolchildren in the Baltimore, Maryland schools. The tests given were the Otis Self-Administered Intelligence Test, the Iowa Reading Test, and the Metropolitan Arithmetic Test (see Shuey, 1958). As it was routinely the case, the white students clearly outperformed the black students, but what was of particular concern was that the African American students appeared to be losing ground in comparison with the white students in terms of academic performance (p. 5).

In his explanation for the dismal (in terms of comparison to whites) performance of the black students, Jenkins emphatically ruled out race as a factor. Instead, he focused on socio-economic status, poor instruction, and inadequate facilities as the culprits. At the end, he makes a recommendation for a thorough analysis of the data and students' social context, and recommends several potential consultants, including his mentor from Northwestern, Paul Witty, to come and provide the expertise required to address the educational needs of the black students.

In viewing Jenkins' (1945) analysis from a socio-cultural perspective, what is immediately striking is how ready all parties were to define African Americans' progress explicitly in terms of how white students were doing.

True, Jenkins did acknowledge socio-economic differences. However, as Canady so skillfully showed, aggregated SES probably lacked enough granularity to tell the real story. African Americans' progress was measured strictly by whether black students were gaining any ground on white students in testing, even though the report acknowledged that in absolute terms of grade level, black students were making their own progress with their proficiencies in their academic subjects (pp. 5-6).

Jenkins' report gives a clear indication of things to come: black students would be assessed, not as Herman Canady (and Alfred Binet) said they should be judged — by how far they had come based on where they were starting from — but by a scale that from a socio-cultural perspective was wholly inappropriate. Countless authors had stated that comparing whites and blacks served little purpose if the aim was the improvement of the black situation. Herman Canady stated clearly that he was most concerned with who his students were and what they had to get done. It was not an issue of whites being "smarter" than blacks. If, as the social factors people claimed, one's position was that the question of racial comparison was suspicious, then it was a waste of time to judge blacks' progress by what whites were doing. However, it speaks to the very essence regarding the importance of an appropriate epistemological perspective that many of the black scholars themselves felt compelled to measure themselves by white standards. As we in this present day know, Jenkins' suggestions would become the primary way that American education has dealt with its "Negro problem." We listened to Martin Jenkins. We did not listen to Herman Canady or Binet.

IN CONCLUSION

The 1945 Jenkins' study is a good place to bring this chapter to a close, because it prepared us for what was to come in the 1950s, 1960s, and beyond. The case against a genetic explanation for intellectual level had to be completely debunked in terms of scholarship, but we still had Arthur Jensen, William Shockley, and the Bell Curve before us. With the exception of Herman Canady, and, perhaps, Otto Klineberg, even the social factors people did not question the concept of a linear measure of intelligence. Yet while the *Journal of Negro Education* was destroying the myth of white superiority with scholarship and methodology, a brilliant Russian psychologist was quietly working on a theory of teaching, learning, and knowing that would take decades to reach the American consciousness. His name was Lev Vygotksy, and he read all of the Western psychologists from Binet to Yerkes. He would become one of the founders of the socio-cultural epistemological perspective of psychology.

It has been my intention to provide an overview of the intelligence testing literature as it pertained to African Americans from 1917 to 1945. I hope that the reader can see what is to me the clear link between the educational practices of that era to those that would follow.

REFERENCES

Alper, T. G., and Boring, E. G. (1944). Intelligence test scores of northern and southern white and Negro recruits in 1918. *Journal of Abnormal and Social Psychology*, 39, 471-474.

Arlitt, A. H. (1921). On the need for caution in establishing race norms. *Journal of Applied Psychology*, 5, 179-183.

Arlitt, A. H. (1922). The relation of intelligence to age in Negro children. *Journal of Applied Psychology*, 6, 378-384.

Beckham, A. S. (1933). A study of the intelligence of colored adolescents of different social-economic status in typical metropolitan areas. *Journal of Social Psychology*, 4, 70-91.

Binet, A. and T. Simon (1916/1973). *The development of intelligence in children (the Binet-Simon scale)*. New York: Arno Press.

Bond, H. M. (1924). Intelligence tests and propaganda. *The Crisis*, 28, 61.

Bond, H. M. (1934). *The education of the Negro in the American social order*. New York: Prentice-Hall Inc.

Bousfield, M. B. (1932). The intelligence and school achievement of Negro children. *Journal of Negro Education*, 1, 388-395.

Brigham, C. C. (1923). *A study of American intelligence*. Oxford, England: Princeton Univ. Press.

Canady, H. G. (1929). Letter from Herman Canady to John Davis dated January 18, 1929. P. John Davis, West Virginia State College. Institute West Virginia, West Virginia State University Library Archives (Herman G. Canady Collection).

Canady, H. G. (1935). Individual differences among freshmen at West Virginia State College. *Journal of Negro Education*, 4, 246-258.

Canady, H. G. (1936a). The effect of "rapport" on the IQ: A new approach to the problem of racial psychology. *Journal of Negro Education*, 5, 209-219.

Canady, H. G. (1936b). The intelligence of Negro college students and parental occupation. *American Journal of Sociology,* 42, 388-389.

Canady, H. G. (1938a). Sex differences in intelligence among Negro college freshmen. *Journal of Applied Psychology,* 22, 437-439.

Canady, H. G. (1938b). Psychology in Negro institutions. *Journal of Negro Education,* 7, 165-171.

Canady, H. G. (1942). The methodology and interpretation of Negro-white mental testing. *School and Society,* 55, 569-575.

Canady, H. G. (1943a). The problem of equating the environment of Negro-white groups for intelligence testing in comparative studies. *Journal of Social Psychology,* 17, 3-15.

Canady, H. G. (1943b). A study of sex differences in intelligence-test scores among 1,306 Negro college freshmen. *Journal of Negro Education,* 12, 167-172.

Canady, H. G., Buxton, C., and Gilliland, A. R. (1942b). A scale for the measurement of the social environment of Negro youth. *Journal of Negro Education,* 11, 4-14.

Clark, R. (1933). The effect of schooling upon intelligence quotients of Negro children. Unpublished doctoral dissertation, Cleveland, Western Reserve University.

Du Bois, W. E. B. (1903). *The Negro problem: A series of articles by representative American Negroes of today.* New York: J. Pott and Company.

Du Bois, W. E. B. (1928). Race relations in the United States. *The Annals fo the American Academy of Political and Social Science,* 140, 6-10.

Editor (1934). Current literature on Negro education. *Journal of Negro Education,* 3, 317.

Fancher, R. E. (1985). *The intelligence men, makers of the IQ controversy.* New York: Norton.

Ferguson, G. O. (1921). Mental status of the American Negro. *Scientific Monthly,* 12, 533-543.

Foreman, C. (1932). *Environmental factors in Negro elementary education.* New York: Norton.

Galton, F. (1869). *Hereditary genius: An inquiry into its laws and consequences.* London: Macmillan and Company.

Galton, F. (1883). *Inquiries into human faculty and its development.* London: Macmillan.

Garth, T. R. (1931). *Race psychology; a study of racial mental differences.* New York: Whittlesey House McGraw-Hill Book Company Inc.

Goddard, H. H. (1920). *Human efficiency and levels of intelligence.* Princeton, NJ: Princeton University Press.

Goodenough, F. L. (1926). Racial differences in the intelligence of school children. *Journal of Experimental Psychology,* 9, 388-397.

Greeno, J. G., Collins, A. M., and Resnick, L. B. (1996). Cognition and learning. In D. Berliner and R. Calfee (Eds.), *Handbook of Educational Psychology* (pp. 15-41). New York: MacMillian.

Guthrie, R. V. (1976). *Even the rat was white: A historical view of psychology.* Boston: Allyn and Bacon.

Herskovits, M. J. (1934). A critical discussion of the "Mulatto Hypothesis." *Journal of Negro Education,* 3, 389-402.

Jenkins, M. D. (1936). A socio-psychological study of Negro children of superior intelligence. *Journal of Negro Education,* 5, 175-190.

Jenkins, M. D. (1939). The mental ability of the American Negro. *Journal of Negro Education,* 7, 511-521.

Jenkins, M. D. (1943). Case studies of Negro children of Binet IQ 160 and above. *Journal of Negro Education,* 12, 159-166.

Jenkins, M. D. (1945). *Interpretation of the semi-annual instructional survey of the Baltimore, Maryland junior and senior high schools September, 1945.* Washington D. C.: Howard University Press.

Klineberg, O. (1928). *An experimental study of speed and other factors in "racial" differences.* New York.

Klneberg, O. (1934). The physical and mental abilities of the American Negro, *The Journal of Negro Education,* 3(3), 478-483.

Klineberg, O. (1935). *Negro intelligence and selective migration.* New York, Columbia University Press.

Lippman, W. (1922a). The mental age of Americans. *New Republic, 32*(412), 213-215.

Lippman, W. (1922b). The mental age of Americans. *New Republic, 32*(414), 275-277.

Long, H. H. (1932). A comparative study of a group of Southern white and Negro infants. *Journal of Negro Education,* 1, 424-427.

Long, H. H. (1934). [Review of the book The effect of schooling upon the intelligence quotients of Negro children]. *Journal of Negro Education,* 3, 136-139.

McAlpin, A. S. (1932). Changes in the intelligence quotients of Negro children. *Journal of Negro Education,* 1, 44-48.

McGraw, M. B. (1931). A comparative study of a group of southern white and Negro infants. *Genetic Psychology Monographs,* 10, 1-105.

Peterson, J. (1923). The comparative abilities of white and Negro children. *Comparative Psychology Monographs, 1*(5), 141.

Price, J. S. C. (1933a). Race and psychology in America [Review of the book race and psychology in America by Thomas Garth]. *Journal of Negro Education,* 2, 83-87.

Price, J. S. C. (1933b). Negro-white differences in achievement. *Journal of Negro Education,* 2, 508-509.

Price, J. S. C. (1934). The physical and mental abilities of the American Negro. *Journal of Negro Education, 3,* 424-452.

Price, J. S. C. (1935). A review of the book Negro intelligence and selective migration by Otto Klneberg. *Journal of Negro Education,* 4, 563-566.

Pyle, W. H. (1915). The mind of the Negro child. *School and Society,* 1, 357-360.

Shuey, A. M. (1958). *The testing of Negro intelligence.* Lynchburg, VA: J.P. Bell Co.

Sims, V. M. (1927). *Sims score card for socio-economic status.* Bloomington, Illinois: Public School Company.

Spencer, J. L. (1992). *Recollections and reflections: A history of the West Virginia State College Psychology department, 1892-1992.* Institute, W. VA: Graphic Arts Production Center West Virginia State College.

Strong, A. C. (1913). Three Hundred Fifty White and Colored Children Measured by the Binet-Simon Measuring Scale of Intelligence. A Comparative Study. *Ped. Sem.,* 20, 485-515.

Sunne, D. (1917). A comparative study of white and Negro children. *Journal of Applied Psychology,* 1, 71-83.

Terman, L. M. (1916,1975). *The measurement of intelligence.* New York: Arno Press.

Thompson, C. H. (1928). The educational achievements of Negro children. *Annals of the American Academy of Political and Social Science,* 140, 193-208.

Thompson, C. H. (1932). Editorial comment: Why a Journal of Negro Education? *Journal of Negro Education,* 1, 1-4.

Thompson, C. H. (1934). The conclusions of scientists relative to racial differences. *Journal of Negro Education,* 3, 494-512.

Thompson, C. H. (1935). The education of the Negro in the American social order. [Review of the education of the Negro in the American social order by Horace Mann Bond]. *Journal of Negro Education,* 4, 266-268.

Thorndike, E. L. (1923). Intelligence scores of colored pupils in high schools. *School and Society,* 18, 569-570.

Whipple, G. M. (1923). The intelligence testing program and its objectors--conscientious and otherwise. *School and Society,* 17, 561-568, 596-604.

Whitney, F. L. (1923). Intelligence levels and school achievement of the white and the colored races in the United States. *Pedagogical Seminary,* 30, 69-86.

Wiggan, G. (2007). Race, school achievement and educational inequality: Towards a student-based inquiry perspective, *Review of Educational Research,* 77(3), 310-333.

Witty, P. A., and Lehman, H. C. (1930). Racial differences: The dogma of superiority. *Journal of Social Psychology,* 1, 394-418.

Witty, P. A., and Jenkins, M. A. (1936). Intra-race testing and Negro intelligence. *Journal of Psychology,* 1, 179-192.

Yerkes, R. M. (Ed.) (1921) *Psychological examining in the United States Army.* Washington, DC: Government Printing Office.

Yoder, D. (1928). Present status of the question of racial differences. *Journal of Educational Psychology,* 19, 463-470.

Young, P. C. (1929). Intelligence and suggestibility in whites and Negroes. *Journal of Comparative Psychology,* 9, 339-359.

ABOUT THE AUTHORS

Sylvie Coulibaly is an Assistant Professor of History at Kenyon College. Her research focuses on the black American intellectual tradition from the Gilded Age to WWII. She received her Ph.D. from Emory University in 2006.

Cameron Seay is currently on the faculty of North Carolina A & T State University in the School of Technology. Seay's bachelor degree is in economics, he has master's degrees in economics, business, and computer information systems, and a doctorate in educational psychology. His current research addresses the school and professional success of African American students.

Greg Wiggan is an Assistant Professor of Urban Education, Adjunct Assistant Professor of Sociology, and Affiliate Faculty Member of Africana Studies at the University of North Carolina at Charlotte. His research addresses history of education, urban education, and urban sociology in the social context of school processes that promote high achievement among African American students and other underserved minority student populations. In doing so, his research also examines the broader connections between the history of urbanization, globalization processes, and the international-ization of education in urban schools. He is co-editor (with Charles Hutchison) of the book, *Global Issues in Education: Pedagogy, Policy, Practice, and the Minority Experience*, and author of *Education in a Strange Land: Globalization, Urbanization, and Urban Schools –The Social and Educational Implications of the Geopolitical Economy*.

INDEX

#

20th century, x, xix, xx, 48
21st century, ix, 64

A

academic performance, 84
access, xv, xvi, 5, 16, 40, 60, 64, 68
accommodation, 47, 48
accounting, 83
acquaintance, 37
activism, 45
adjustment, 50
administrators, 10, 16, 23
adolescents, 71, 86
advancement, xvi, xx, 33, 34, 37, 48
advancements, 2
Africa, xi, xiii, xiv, xvi, xvii, xviii, xix, xxii, xxiii, 5, 11
African Americans , xiv, xvi, xvii, xviii, xix, xx, xxi, 1, 2, 3, 4, 8, 10, 13, 14, 15, 21, 24, 25, 26, 30, 31, 32, 33, 34, 35, 46, 53, 54, 55, 56, 57, 59, 60, 61, 62, 63, 64, 65, 67, 68, 69, 70, 71, 72, 73, 75, 76, 77, 80, 81, 83, 84, 86
age, 58, 60, 67, 69, 70, 76, 86

agriculture, 7
American Missionary Association, xix, xx, xxii, 1, 4, 29
ancestors, xv, xviii
anger, 44
Anglican Church, xvii
anthropologists, 72, 73, 74, 78
anthropology, 73, 77, 80, 81
appraisals, 65
appropriations, 9, 23
Archibald Grimke, 42
arithmetic, 64
assault, 34, 77, 82, 83
assessment, xxi, 53, 63, 65, 66, 71, 72, 77
Atlanta Cotton States Exposition, 34
Atlanta Exposition, 31
Atlanta University, x, xix, xx, xxii, 1, 2, 6, 8, 11, 12, 13, 15, 22, 24, 26, 27, 28, 29, 48
attachment, 43
authority, xii, xvii
awareness, 54

B

Barbados, ix
Barry Chevannes, ix, xvii
Bible, xii, xvii, xviii, 10
Birmingham, Alabama, 70
Black Education, 4, 31

black intellectuals, xx, 33, 34, 35, 45
black intelligentsia, 33, 40, 42, 45
black tea, 14, 15, 47, 48
black women, 15, 16
blacks, xix, 32
blood, xiii, xvi, 56, 57, 58, 59, 74
Booker T. Washington, xxi, 25, 31, 32, 34,
    35, 37, 42, 43, 44, 45, 46, 47, 48, 49, 50
breakdown, 73

C

catalyst, 35
Catholic Church, xii, xiv, xv, xvi, xvii
Catholics, xvi
certification, 47
challenges, xix, 3, 8
Chicago, 28, 30, 49, 60, 61, 66, 73, 76, 77,
    81
children, xiv, xix, 4, 6, 9, 14, 15, 17, 22, 23,
    26, 37, 44, 46, 55, 57, 60, 61, 62, 66, 67,
    70, 76, 86, 87, 88, 89
Chile, x
Christianity, x, xv, xxii, 11
cities, 47, 71
citizenship, xxi, 31, 33, 34, 39, 42, 46
city, 30, 41, 70
civil rights, 33, 34, 36
Civil War, xviii, xx, 3, 4, 8, 24, 33
civilization, xi, 27, 28, 39, 46
classes, 17, 20, 22, 47, 60
classification, 12
classroom, 13, 16, 24
climate, 8, 16, 25, 81
clinical psychology, 78
college students, 48, 87
colleges, xix, 4, 7, 8, 10, 16, 21, 28, 30, 57,
    77, 78, 79
colonization, xii, xiv, xvii
color, xxiii, 35, 49, 83
Committee of Twelve, 42, 43, 45
common sense, 48, 55, 64

communities, 30
community, 2, 3, 9, 15, 20, 39, 57, 58, 81,
    82
compilation, 71
complexity, 32
composition, 8, 20, 74
conciliation, 44
conditioning, 61
conference, xvii, 41, 42, 43
conflict, 45
Congress, 3
consciousness, 85
consensus, 45, 84
consent, xiii
Constitution, 11
construction, 75
control group, 69, 70
controlled studies, 70
controversial, xxi
conviction, 47
cooperation, 44
correlation, 63, 70, 82
cotton, 8, 34
covering, 17
critical analysis, 67
criticism, 8, 12, 40, 45, 46
cultural differences, 72
cultural norms, 12
cultural values, 13
culture, xvi, xvii, xviii, 13, 22, 23, 36, 38, 58
curricula, 12, 13, 79
curriculum, xx, 1, 10, 11, 12, 13, 25, 78

D

danger, 39
decolonization, xiii, xviii
democracy, 29
Democratic Party, 49
depth, 37
destiny, 10
dichotomy, 32

disappointment, xi, 24
discrimination, xiv, xvii, 16, 45
distribution, 64
District of Columbia, 66, 71
divergence, 58
diversity, xiv, 44
donations, 4, 25, 26, 78
donors, 25
dream, 35

E

economic progress, xxi, 46
economic status, 58, 61, 79, 82, 83, 84, 86, 89
economics, 78
editors, 40
education, ix, x, xi, xiv, xv, xvi, xviii, xix, xx, xxi, xxii, xxiii, 1, 2, 3, 4, 5, 6, 8, 9, 10, 11, 12, 13, 14, 15, 16, 18, 21, 23, 24, 25, 26, 27, 28, 29, 30, 31, 32, 33, 34, 35, 36, 37, 38, 39, 40, 41, 43, 44, 45, 46, 47, 48, 49, 50, 53, 54, 56, 57, 59, 60, 62, 64, 65, 66, 67, 68, 69, 73, 75, 76, 77, 78, 80, 81, 85, 86, 87, 89
educational practices, 86
educational psychology, 61, 62, 75
educational research, 66, 71, 72
educational system, xix, 53
educators, vii, xxi, 14, 15, 16, 17, 38, 53, 54, 78
Egypt, 11
elementary school, 76
empowerment, 32
engineering, 38
England, xvii, 86
enrollment, 6, 15, 16
enslavement, xv, 37
environment, xxi, 55, 56, 58, 59, 60, 61, 66, 70, 77, 78, 81, 87
environmental factors, 59
equality, 5, 23, 29, 31, 32, 35, 47, 48

equipment, 9
Europe, 81, 82
evidence, 58, 68, 73, 74, 80
evil, 39
evolution, 54
examinations, 8, 63
exclusion, 23
exercise, 38
expertise, 74, 84
exposure, 66

F

faith, 43
families, 9, 54, 76
FAS, 7
fear, xiv, xvi, 37, 41, 42, 45
fears, 42
feelings, 24, 40
fights, 34
financial, 6, 19, 31
financial support, 19
flaws, 55, 58, 77
food, 78
force, xi, xiii, xv, xxi, 10, 25, 43, 53, 67, 79
formation, 42
formula, 69
foundations, 54, 74
freedom, xiii, xv, xviii, xx, 1, 2, 3, 4, 17, 29, 30
friendship, 37
funding, 9, 25, 45, 65
funds, 3, 6, 10, 23, 24

G

gender differences, 79, 83
gender role, 17
genetics, xxi, 56
geography, 8, 83
geometry, 8

Georgia, x, xx, xxii, 1, 2, 3, 4, 6, 7, 9, 10, 13, 15, 16, 17, 18, 19, 20, 21, 23, 24, 26, 27, 28, 29, 30
gifted, 30, 76, 77, 83
Gilded Age, xx, 31, 32, 36
God, xiii, xv, xvii
Gold Coast of Africa, xii
governor, 23
grades, 66, 76
graduate program, 57
graduate students, 57
group identity, 37
group variance, 79
guardian, 49
guidance, 1
guidelines, 23
gunpowder, xi

H

Haiti, x, xiii, xv
heredity, xxi, 56
high school, 8, 75, 88, 89
higher education, xix, xx, 2, 4, 6, 8, 9, 10, 11, 12, 13, 14, 23, 24, 25, 28, 29, 31, 35, 38, 39, 43, 46
history, ix, x, xi, xvi, xvii, xix, xx, xxi, xxii, xxiii, 2, 8, 11, 20, 24, 26, 27, 28, 29, 37, 39, 49, 50, 89
homes, 83
host, 63
House, xxiii, 18, 29, 87
human, xv, xvi, xvii, xxi, 39, 71, 75, 87
hypothesis, xiii, 56, 70, 74

I

ideal, 60
ideals, 11, 12, 39, 48, 81
ideology, xiii, xiv, xxii, 9, 11, 48
illusion, 23
improvements, 2

in transition, 27, 28
income, 81
independence, ix, xiii, xv
Indians, 58
individual differences, 79
individuals, 1, 17
indoctrination, xii, xvii
industrial studies, 9
inequality, xvi, 30, 90
infants, 88
inferiority, 21, 37, 60, 61, 62, 73, 77
injure, 37
injury, iv
institutions, xix, 1, 5, 7, 9, 10, 17, 21, 28, 29, 32, 39, 47, 48, 50, 87
integration, 5, 23, 49
integrity, 44
intellect, 74
intelligence, xiv, xix, xxi, 53, 54, 55, 56, 57, 58, 59, 60, 61, 63, 64, 65, 66, 67, 69, 70, 72, 74, 75, 76, 77, 79, 80, 81, 82, 83, 84, 85, 86, 87, 88, 89, 90
Iowa, 84
IQ, 60, 66, 67, 69, 70, 72, 76, 79, 83, 86, 87, 88
irony, xvi, 41
issues, 11, 12, 43, 64, 65

J

Jamaica, vii, ix, xi, xv, xvii, xxii

L

labor market, 46
landscape, xvi, 15
languages, xvii, 11, 12, 13, 21
laws, xviii, 39, 87
lead, 75
leadership, x, 39, 42, 47, 48
leadership style, 42

learning, xvi, xvii, xviii, xx, 1, 4, 7, 8, 9, 10, 22, 35, 36, 37, 39, 41, 53, 85, 88
legs, 72
lens, 64
level of education, 62, 63, 83
liberation theology, xvii
lifetime, 32
light, xiii, xxi, 16, 29, 66, 68, 77
literacy, 5
Louisiana, 50, 73, 82
love, vii, x, 24, 29

M

magnitude, 63
majority, xvii, xviii, 8, 14, 17, 22, 38, 73
man, 13, 32, 35, 36, 39, 41, 45, 49
manual education, 9, 21
manufacturing, 39
Maryland, 71, 84, 88
masking, xix
mass, 34, 54, 55, 57
materialism, 41
mathematics, 8, 75
matter, 41, 72, 80
measurement, 58, 68, 69, 72, 77, 82, 87, 89
meat, 39
median, 66, 76
medical, 3, 18
medicine, 18, 29
membership, 44
memory, 6
mental ability, 61, 74, 88
mental age, 56, 58, 64, 67, 88
mentor, 59, 76, 84
messages, xiv
methodology, 68, 85, 87
metropolitan areas, 86
middle class, xxii, 16, 17, 29
migrants, 70
migration, 57, 70, 74, 88, 89
minority students, 53

mission, 7, 9, 15, 24, 50, 67
Missouri, 26, 30
momentum, 72
moral code, 78
morality, 13
mortality, 13
motivation, 58
Mulatto Hypothesis, 56, 58, 59, 71, 74, 77, 88
music, xvii, xxii, 19

N

National Center for Education Statistics, 29
Nazi Germany, 80
New England, 10, 13
next generation, 80

O

objectivity, 71
opportunities, xix, 15, 24, 33, 48, 61
oppression, 37
organize, 65
overtime, 69

P

parents, x, 9, 34, 72, 76
participants, 55, 73
personality, 45
Philadelphia, 13, 26, 28
plaque, 6
platform, 41, 45
playing, 36
poetry, 55
policy, 41
politics, xx, 23, 25
population, xv, 23, 38, 47, 70, 71, 76
portfolio, 80
poverty, xx, 35, 66
pragmatism, 48

prejudice, vii, 13
preparation, iv, 41, 46
preservation, xvi, 10
presidency, 62
president, x, 6, 17, 20, 23, 24, 36, 39, 43, 44, 48, 78
President, x, 5, 6, 10, 13, 21, 24, 28, 29, 34, 44, 78
prestige, 16
prima facie, 57
primary function, 37
primary school, 22
principles, xvi, 43, 48
private schools, 1, 48
probability, 59
project, 1, 83
propaganda, 86
proposition, 33, 37, 64, 73
prosperity, 24
psychologist, 71, 81, 85
psychology, 53, 54, 57, 60, 62, 63, 64, 73, 74, 75, 76, 77, 78, 79, 80, 81, 86, 87, 88, 89
public education, 35
public schools, xxii, 9, 14, 55
punishment, 23

Q

questioning, xii

R

race, xvii, xxii, 5, 12, 13, 16, 22, 23, 24, 25, 29, 30, 33, 34, 35, 36, 37, 38, 39, 40, 41, 45, 46, 47, 48, 49, 50, 55, 56, 58, 59, 64, 66, 67, 71, 72, 73, 74, 79, 80, 81, 82, 83, 84, 86, 89, 90
racial differences, 59, 89, 90
racial minorities, 75
racism, vii, 34
radicalism, xxii

rash, 45
reading, xviii, 76
reality, 28, 35
reasoning, 57
recalling, 12
recognition, ix, 25
recommendations, 79
reconciliation, 45
reconstruction, 28, 30
Reconstruction Period, 1
reform, xix, xxii, 23, 29, 50
Reform, xx, 2
reforms, 39, 42
reinforcement, 72
relevance, 65, 81
reliability, 82
Republican Party, 49
reputation, 59, 72
requirements, 21
researchers, ix, xi, 21, 56, 57, 60, 66, 69, 71, 75, 77
resentment, 44
resistance, 5, 48, 50
resources, 4, 5, 6, 9
response, xiv, 23, 58
retaliation, 45
rights, xviii, 23, 31, 39, 40
risk, 32, 64
Roman Catholic Church, xii, xvi, xvii
Roosevelt, Theodore, 44
roots, xviii, xxii, 27
rural areas, 47
rural schools, 16

S

sadness, 37
sarcasm, 60
scarcity, 4
schema, 32
scholarship, xxi, 85
scholastic achievement, 61

Scholastic Aptitude Test, 55
school, xiv, xvi, xviii, xix, xx, 3, 4, 5, 6, 7, 8, 9, 10, 12, 13, 14, 15, 16, 17, 18, 20, 22, 23, 24, 26, 30, 38, 39, 47, 48, 53, 57, 59, 61, 62, 63, 65, 66, 68, 70, 72, 75, 76, 84, 86, 88, 90
schooling, 12, 26, 44, 58, 82, 87, 88
science, xxi, 8, 64
scientific validity, 57
scope, 17
secondary schools, 6, 47
second-class citizens, 3
segregation, xvii, 23, 28, 31, 32, 67, 82
self-esteem, 38
self-worth, 37
services, 3
SES, 76, 79, 81, 82, 85
settlements, 13
sex, 87
sex differences, 87
shelter, 26
shock, 40
shock waves, 40
silver, 19
single test, 53
skin, xiv, 56, 83
slavery, xii, xv, xvi, xxiii, 3, 4, 8, 11, 29, 30, 51
slaves, ix, xi, xii, xiii, xiv, xv, xvi, xx, 3, 4, 13, 14, 15, 17, 24, 26
smallpox, xi
social class, xiii, xx, 2, 17, 23
social context, 53, 72, 78, 81, 82, 84
social environment, 87
social hierarchy, xiii, 57
social movements, 39
social order, 17, 27, 86, 89
social problems, 38
social sciences, 54, 80
social status, 56, 59
social structure, 77
society, ix, xiii, xiv, xvi, 7, 35, 65, 75, 77, 81, 82

socioeconomic status, 70, 72
sociology, 11, 13, 26, 34, 64, 73, 78, 80
Socrates, 41
solution, 34
South Africa, 28
specialization, 64
species, 71
speech, 34, 36
spirituality, xiv, xix, 5
standard error, 69
standardized testing, xix, 55
state, xx, 1, 4, 9, 16, 17, 18, 19, 24, 64, 75, 77, 79, 83
states, xiii, 12, 16, 47, 84
statistics, xix
steel, 41
stratification, 61
structural barriers, 16
structure, xx, 2, 35
student achievement, xix
style, xvii, 10, 25, 68, 69
Styles, 20
subscribers, 45

T

talent, 32
teachers, 4, 5, 8, 15, 16, 22, 23, 24, 29, 30, 36, 38, 47, 76
tension, 44, 45
test scores, 66, 68, 69, 79, 82, 86, 87
testing, xiv, xix, xxi, 54, 55, 57, 60, 70, 81, 82, 85, 86, 87, 89, 90
testing program, 90
trade, ix, xi, xii, 39
training, xix, 8, 9, 11, 12, 13, 22, 24, 25, 38, 39, 44, 46, 47, 53, 61, 63, 64, 67
translation, 55
treatment, xi, 57

                                   Index

U

United, xxiii, 17, 49, 64, 80, 87, 90
universities, xix, 4, 7, 11, 21, 28, 65, 74, 79
urban, xx, 16, 26, 30, 91
urbanization, xx, 13

V

variable factor, 77
vein, 83
venue, 43
Viking, 29
vision, 6, 24, 36, 38, 75
vocational education, 9
vocational training, 4, 25
vote, 42, 45

W

war, xvii, 3, 41, 82
Washington, xix, xxi, 25, 29, 31, 32, 33, 34,
   35, 36, 37, 38, 39, 40, 41, 42, 43, 44, 45,
   46, 47, 48, 49, 50, 51, 55, 63, 71, 78, 88,
   90
waste, 40, 85
watershed, 40, 75
wealth, xi, xii, 39
wear, 43
West Africa, x, xviii, 11
white Southerners, 34
white supremacist ideology, xiii, xiv
withdrawal, 43
workers, 35
World War I, xxi, 31, 32, 80
worldwide, 65

Y

Yale University, xix, 13
young people, 10

Z

Zulu, xiii